"Dr. Mark Strong is an example of stre community, even serving on our bo produced a book to help strengthen

significant changes. *Who Moved My Neighborhood?* acknowledges the pain and sorrow that can come with a changing neighborhood, provides keys for processing through it, and offers incredible guidance and practical steps for trusting God for the future. Any faith-based community facing the impacts of gentrification or economic change will be inspired, encouraged, and energized by the wisdom and shared journey present in *Who Moved My Neighborhood?*"
Judah Smith, lead pastor of Churchome, Kirkland, Washington

"As someone who witnessed the slow gentrification process around Life Change Church, and as someone who heard the deep soul-searching conversations the pastors and leaders had, I urge every church leader to read this book. If this isn't happening to you, it's surely happening to a church nearby, and if this is happening to you, Pastor Strong's practical leadership principles and warm spiritual wisdom will guide your church to a future with healing and hope."
MaryKate Morse, author and executive dean, Portland Seminary

"My friend Mark Strong and his folks at Life Change Church have navigated the struggles of gentrification here in Portland, Oregon, and have done so with grace and prophetic vision. *Who Moved My Neighborhood?* offers practical and faithful insights for churches struggling with the inevitable challenges that develop as our communities change. Healing, hope, and great impact are possible!"
Kevin Palau, president of the Luis Palau Association

"US census data shows ethnic diversity increasing almost everywhere in the country. One key exception is urban areas of most large cities that have been historically African American, which are seeing a dramatic increase in their White population. This return to the city has brought escalating rental rates and property taxes, forcing longtime residents to find new homes outside the cities. These shifts take a great toll on the churches that have been the heart and soul of these communities. Dr. Mark Strong has pastored one of those churches in Portland, Oregon—the most gentrified city in America. He has learned ways to navigate the change in his neighborhood that have enabled Life Change Church to help change the lives of both the gentrifiers moving into the city and the longtime attenders who made their way to the suburbs. Strong has coached other churches with these principles, enabling them to stay on mission even when their neighborhood moved. If you are a pastor in a neighborhood whose residents are moving or want to gain life principles for navigating change, this book is for you."
Alan Ehler, dean of Southeastern University's Barnett College of Ministry and Theology, author of *How to Make Big Decisions Wisely*

"A timely and prophetic word on the ongoing injustices of race and place in America, from one of the most recognized leaders on the subject of gentrification."

Ken Wytsma, author of *The Myth of Equality: Uncovering the Roots of Injustice and Privilege*

"While America marathon watched *Portlandia*, I watched as Mark and other Black pastors in our city worked tirelessly to shepherd a community that was being displaced. In order to create the myth of *Portlandia*, thousands of people of color had to be moved out, left to grieve their loss of place and community. Sadly, gentrification is happening all across America, leaving countless pastors and churches asking, 'What do we do?' I am so thankful Mark wrote this book, because not only has he led his church well through this massive upheaval, he has done it through healing hearts, dreaming new dreams, and bringing renewed hope."

Rick McKinley, lead pastor of Imago Dei Community, Portland, Oregon

"Mark Strong is without a doubt one of the most respected, trusted leaders here in Portland. He's a deep well of wisdom and insight into the changing dynamics of urban ministry. This book will be an extraordinary help to many."

John Mark Comer, author of *Live No Lies* and *The Ruthless Elimination of Hurry*

"Jesus calls all who call him Lord to embrace a lifestyle of neighborly love. With humble transparency and helpful practical wisdom, Mark Strong makes a compelling case that loving our neighbor means loving our neighborhood, even when it goes through dramatic demographic and economic change. I believe every Christian leader ought to read this important book, not only for greater understanding in navigating the challenging terrain of a moved neighborhood but also for a fresh vision of God and his redemptive mission of love in the world. I highly recommend it."

Tom Nelson, author of *The Flourishing Pastor* and president of Made to Flourish

"Mark Strong helps us get our arms around a challenging issue that perplexes community leaders across the country. With insight born of experience and wisdom seasoned with grace, he provides navigational understanding and guidance that will be helpful to everyone touched by changing neighborhoods and by all who are committed to community flourishing."

Steve Moore, CEO of M. J. Murdock Charitable Trust

MARK E. STRONG

WHO MOVED MY

FOREWORD BY
HAROLD
CALVIN RAY

NEIGHBORHOOD

?

LEADING CONGREGATIONS THROUGH GENTRIFICATION AND ECONOMIC CHANGE

ivp

An imprint of InterVarsity Press
Downers Grove, Illinois

InterVarsity Press
P.O. Box 1400, Downers Grove, IL 60515-1426
ivpress.com
email@ivpress.com

InterVarsity Press® is the book-publishing division of InterVarsity Christian Fellowship/USA®, a movement of students and faculty active on campus at hundreds of universities, colleges, and schools of nursing in the United States of America, and a member movement of the International Fellowship of Evangelical Students. For information about local and regional activities, visit intervarsity.org.

Scripture taken from the New King James Version®. Copyright © 1982 by Thomas Nelson. Used by permission. All rights reserved.

While any stories in this book are true, some names and identifying information may have been changed to protect the privacy of individuals.

Published in association with Jenni Burke of Illuminate Literary Agency: www.illuminateliterary.com.

The publisher cannot verify the accuracy or functionality of website URLs used in this book beyond the date of publication.

Cover design and image composite: David Fassett
Interior design: Daniel van Loon
Images: steps of a scaffold: © acilo / iStock / Getty Images
  prairie church: © Joanna McCarthy / The Image Bank / Getty Images
  colorful, ripped grunge paper: © NikolaVukojevic / iStock / Getty Images
  black and white grunge paper: © NikolaVukojevic / iStock / Getty Images
  historic brick wall: © omersukrugoksu / E+ / Getty Images
  construction crane: © ROBOTOK / iStock / Getty Images
  rough textured pearl white paper: © tomograf / E+ / Getty Images

ISBN 978-1-5140-0238-4 (print)
ISBN 978-1-5140-0239-1 (digital)

Printed in the United States of America ♾

InterVarsity Press is committed to ecological stewardship and to the conservation of natural resources in all our operations. This book was printed using sustainably sourced paper.

Library of Congress Cataloging-in-Publication Data
A catalog record for this book is available from the Library of Congress.

P	25	24	23	22	21	20	19	18	17	16	15	14	13	12	11	10	9	8	7	6	5	4	3	2	1
Y	42	41	40	39	38	37	36	35	34	33	32	31	30	29	28	27	26	25	24	23	22				

This book is affectionately dedicated to the

Life Change Church family—

*for your resiliency, determination, and faith
in the Lord Jesus Christ,
for your faithfulness in continuing to be the church
even though the neighborhood around you has moved.*

And to the many churches

*that find themselves in a different neighborhood
though they have not moved.*

CONTENTS

Foreword by Harold Calvin Ray—*1*

Preface—*7*

PART 1—NAVIGATING THE HEALING PROCESS

1 Who Moved My Neighborhood?—*11*

2 Discovering the Healing Process—*18*

3 Regular—*23*

4 Recognition—*30*

5 Realization—*39*

6 Reconstruction—*51*

7 Rage—*58*

8 Reconciliation—*66*

PART 2—MAPPING YOUR FUTURE

9 Revamp—*85*

10 The Vision Question—*93*

11 The Identity Question—*104*

12 The Purpose Question—*117*

13 The Relational Question—*127*

14 Navigational Surprises—*134*

Conclusion—*142*

Appendix: Relational Jump Starters—*147*

Navigation Guide: Discussion Questions—*160*

Notes—*165*

Scripture Index—*168*

FOREWORD

Harold Calvin Ray

Every once and again, there arises from the midst of the rancorous clamor and passionate outcry of those who protest against recognized but curable social injustices and economic inequities a distinctive voice speaking with clarity, precision, and pragmatism in an effort to assuage the repetitive rehearsals of the obvious by presenting effective, solution-oriented alternatives to those wrestling with the issues at hand. Escaping for the moment the hearty temptation to prolong the exercise of bemoaning and lamenting, this voice chooses to light a candle of hope even while cursing the darkness of the communal despair.

Writing with remarkable and deliberate transparency, buttressed by his experiential credibility, Dr. Mark Strong in his timely and prophetic work *Who Moved My Neighborhood?* presents his foot soldier contemporaries in pastoral ministry with a revelatory self-help manual. This powerful treatise promotes and expedites a healing and reconciliation process for those pastors who find themselves facing the conundrum of anger, fear, and frustration. These emotional extremes are the understandable result of pastors being encumbered with the indelible challenge of leading what remains of a dispersed congregation into meaningful engagement with a neighborhood that they no longer recognize.

A 2020 national report titled *Never More Urgent: A Preliminary Review of How the U.S. is leaving Black, Hispanic and Indigenous Communities Behind* from the National Center for Faith-Based Initiatives noted that the identification and elimination of the policies, practices, and preferences that have historically, socially, and economically disenfranchised communities of color were a foremost but essential challenge of our modern-day society. This, of course, indicates that we are seriously interested in affirmatively addressing the glaring disparity across all spectrums of quality of life indices created by those policies, practices, and preferences.

The report further noted that the irrefutable disproportionate effect of Covid-19 on communities of color, when superimposed on already existing policy disparities, further demonstrated the dramatic quality of life gap experienced by minority communities. As such, the pandemic essentially served as a floodlight illuminating a myriad of debilitating maladies strangling the sustainable development of Black, Brown, and Indigenous communities.

However, while the Covid-19 pandemic rightfully focused media and governmental attention on the impact felt across all sectors of community life, another more historically rooted malady that dramatically and adversely affects the longevity, vitality, and sustainability of communities continues to run its course through the veins of communities of color in many of our nation's largest cities. Gentrification serves to disrupt community life as it had been known and displaces a community's commonwealth of historically rooted family trees, which had been responsible for fomenting dynamic, entrepreneurial, and "front porch"–oriented community life.

It is clear that gentrification in and of itself need not necessarily be a bad thing. Every community needs change and must change as we encounter the white water rapids of cultural and societal change, as well as technological connectivity in our world. That stated, gentrification is only a good thing when the resulting *evolution* of the community does not simultaneously and inherently mean the *elimination* of that community!

Inner city development with such avarice and malevolent intent critically devalues the community that "was" with a presumptive and tragically flawed conclusion that the historic and passionate stakeholders of that community need not be consulted in the redesign nor included in the economic benefits and entrepreneurial opportunities resulting from that redesign. As Jane Jacobs warned nearly sixty years ago in her work titled *The Death and Life of Great American Cities*, such a flood of investment capital into reshaping historical neighborhoods according to the whims of outside forces is "no constructive way to nurture cities."[1]

Daniel Herriges, senior editor of *Strong Towns*, aptly notes that unfortunately "concentrated poverty and its mirror image, concentrated affluence, are at historic highs. And our neighborhoods are caught between a destructive pair of outcomes: either experience stagnation and slow decay, or a cascade of redevelopment that leaves a place scoured of its former identity." He continues, "We need to retool our regulatory processes and financing systems to legalize small. Right now, convoluted zoning and development rules, long and uncertain approval processes, and financing mechanisms that favor predictability and standardization have left an oligopoly of deep pocketed developers as nearly the only ones who can afford to be in the game. This precludes many citizens from playing a meaningful role in co-creating the places they will live. And it is at the root of America's overlapping housing and affordability crises."[2]

Indeed, Herriges argues, "I think a principle of a good neighborhood should be that those who want to stay can stay. It's not that neighborhoods shouldn't change or that they are 'owned' by one ethnic or demographic group. It's about the intangible benefits of social capital and community stability, which are washed away when the makeup of the community is in dramatic flux."[3]

Alas, the issue of radically changed neighborhoods through gentrification is the precise intersection now being faced by pastors across our nation, as Strong splendidly addresses in this work. Noting appropriately that change was not the issue as much as non-inclusion in the change was the problem, Strong uses his depth of experiential exposures and resulting practical wisdom to encourage his contemporaries in pastoral ministry to arise from fear and despair. He wisely advises pastors to strategically engage their changing circumstances, beginning with prayerfully reconnecting to the "missional, visional, and relational" calling of themselves personally and of the church corporately.

Who Moved My Neighborhood? is remarkable for its warm, personable, yet instructive guidance. Pastors are repetitively reminded that their pain is not their address, but rather an essential part of a seven phased process of recognition, realization, reconstruction, and reconciliation among other critical factors. In doing so, Strong masterfully blends episodes of personal encounter with such dilemmas as momentarily getting lost within his lifelong community, finding street intersections unrecognizable, and vestiges of the community such as landmark eateries in which he grew, lived, and loved now replaced by gleaming but unwelcoming live here–work here structures.

His masterful reference to the lament of those who could no longer sing by the rivers of Babylon is as informing to the pastors he seeks to encourage across the country as it is reflective of the unique gifting and anointing with which he has been graced as a pastor and leader within his community.

One can all but sense the reality of the inevitable fate of psychic devaluation as he describes the moment of his self-actualized experience of sharing with glee the memories of what the community "was" with a neighborhood tour group that he readily discerned had little concern or value attributed to anything but that which "is" now. Yet Strong asserts that a major element of coping with the reality of change is the privilege and importance of remembering. This, he argues, is the touchstone of identity and validation so essential to the healing process. To this, he adds an effective Nehemiah prototype of coping, regrouping, and rebuilding within the confines of a changed community while harnessing power, and trusting the prophetic mandate and spiritual authority of an unchanged calling!

In the final analysis, this unction as urged by Strong as a central tenet of *Who Moved My Neighborhood?* must be the sustaining factor and the futuristic catalyst for every pastor who trusts God for stability in the midst of mandated mobility, and for resonance without dilution of relevance. Indeed, more than fifty years ago, Dr. Martin Luther King Jr. said, "Any religion that professes to be concerned about the souls of men and is not concerned about economic conditions that cripple them and the social conditions that damn them is a dry as dust religion in need of new blood."[4]

That prophetic mandate still rests on the shoulders of pastors near and far. We are never to be exempted from the process. We are too essential to the process. Accordingly, as Strong urges, we must pick up the mantle of proactive engagement of public policy and collective engagement of the processes by which change occurs right before our eyes. Thanks to Strong, however, we are reminded that such an engagement begins with clarion attention to the conversations ensuing in, around, and about the communities we love and serve.

It remains our mandate to provide a spiritual and practical continuum of purpose-driven services and leadership that will strategically lead toward the dignity of an affordable yet higher quality of life for the constituencies and communities we serve.

Thanks to Strong and his insightful, encouraging, and enlightening work, we now have a practical tool to buttress our spiritual authority and a prophetic mandate to accomplish that task, even amid a sea of societal and neighborhood change.

PREFACE

Throughout our nation many neighborhoods are moving. These shifts can result from economic growth or decline, gentrification, or other geographical changes. These changes bring with them a mixed bag of emotions, perspectives, and opportunities. For some, the changing neighborhood becomes the new "promised land," the turf of fresh opportunity—an old space made new, filled with chic, artsy, and trendy hotspots. They become the electric place with the "buzz," where people come from across the state and the nation to "vibe." They are the compelling new oases where a whole new demographic wants to live and be.

But for the longtime residents of those neighborhoods, the sentiments are vastly different. With the rapid emergence of new developments, businesses, and residences, they lament as they watch the fingerprints left by past generations on their beloved community vanish as neighborhood revitalization progresses. As their semblance disappears, they feel unwanted, powerless, and insignificant in a neighborhood that for years has been their home.

The church is not exempt from these difficult neighborhood shifts. When a local church has loved and served its community for years and, suddenly, becomes strangers in its own neighborhood, the challenges are great. Its new reality forces it to change internally and externally. How the church navigates these changes determines if it will live, die, or be reduced to a tragic existence on life support.

Navigating a new neighborhood is complex. It requires the church to deliberately take the time to process the new changes, to grieve, and to heal. It also requires a revamping, where the church must courageously look at itself in the mirror and ask difficult, heart-probing questions that will cause some discomfort—transformational questions that will require hard work to answer. Enmeshed in the process as well is the task of discerning God's will, a reconciling of sorts that suggests that in the unwanted (or maybe wanted) changes our neighborhoods have undergone, God may be up to something new. This process also involves coming to grips with the truth that the newness may require our churches to change in order to reengage our neighborhoods in a redemptive manner—or perhaps choose another option.

My purpose in writing this book is to compassionately help pastors, leaders, and churches *faithfully* navigate the treacherous terrain of a changing neighborhood—a moved neighborhood. This is not a book about gentrification per se, but it will show you how our church has navigated some of the difficulties inevitably brought on by gentrification in our city in order to share what we've learned so far in our process. And, for the record, by no means have we arrived! I'm not writing as an expert or a guru who has it all figured out but as a fellow sojourner serving Christ and his church in a moved neighborhood.

My prayer for you is that this book will help you and your church—your board, your pastors and leaders, and the members of your congregation—in your navigational process. I'm also hoping you will discover that, regardless of what's transpiring in the changing community around you, God still has a great purpose for your church. With his divine assistance, you can help navigate your church into an exciting future in an old but new neighborhood.

PART 1

NAVIGATING THE HEALING PROCESS

CHAPTER 1

WHO MOVED MY NEIGHBORHOOD?

I'll admit my bias up front: I think Life Change Church is an awesome local church. We are a racially diverse church with wonderful people who love one another and are seeking to initiate what I call a "divine merger" between the work of the church and the work of Christ in our city for Jesus. My wife, Marla, and I have been serving as the lead pastors of Life Change Church since 1988, and over the years we, along with our congregation, have experienced a myriad of joys, pains, and sorrows. However, we've never experienced anything that has impacted our church quite as much as figuring out how to navigate our church in a radically different neighborhood. For everyone who is a part of Life Change, the struggle is long, painful at times, and exasperating. And, if I'm being honest, sometimes we feel hopeless.

Since the early 1960s our church has been located in the heart of North and Northeast Portland, Oregon—in the neighborhood formerly known as "the

Hood." For years this neighborhood had been home to the majority of African Americans living in Oregon. In the Hood, our church's first building was a small A-frame structure tucked away in a hidden cul-de-sac on Ivy Street. It was a simple rustic structure where many precious "God moments" were woven into our hearts by the Holy Spirit. In fact, it was in this sacred space that I personally came to faith in Christ. In 1996, we purchased an old shopping complex and moved our church to its current home. During those years the only moving our church had to deal with was geographical—and it was just a four-block journey!

A few years back, giving directions to our church was a cinch. All we had to say was, "It's the big building between Williams Avenue and Vancouver, one block south of Fremont Street. You can't miss it!" But nowadays directions require a bit more explanation, or else people will drive past the church. It's amazing to think at one time our building was the largest structure on our block—you couldn't miss it. But now, our building is dwarfed by several new developments.

Our church is not the only entity hidden by the changes that have occurred in our neighborhood. Over the last fifteen years, many other beloved fixtures have not just been hidden but have been gone forever. This is a reality that is hard to come to terms with. While all neighborhoods shift over time, there are some scenarios that accelerate these shifts—sometimes at a pace so rapid that we don't even see the change coming.

MISSING PERSONS

I was born at Emmanuel Hospital, only several blocks from our church. Until age four or five, my family, which at the time consisted of my father, my mother, and me, lived less than a half a mile from the church I currently pastor and the hospital where I was born. My grandparents on both my mother's and father's sides lived only a short walking distance away from us as well. All my aunts, uncles, and cousins were close too. When my father landed a different job, we moved to Bellevue, Washington, where we lived for about twelve years. However, every holiday vacation, every summer, and in every other window of opportunity, we traveled to Portland. It was our home away from home.

My sophomore year in high school, our family moved back to Northeast Portland for good. Even though we had visited frequently, moving back was a culture shock for me. Bellevue had been predominately White—our family was pretty much the only Black family in the neighborhood. My brother and I and two or three others were the only Black kids in the elementary school, in the junior high school, on the sports teams, and so on. In fact, we were the only Black family in the church we attended. Northeast Portland was drastically different.

In our new home, African American people were our next-door neighbors. Hundreds of Black kids went to the school we attended. On our sports teams, at least three quarters of our teammates were Black and Brown kids. And we also competed against teams with similar demographics. If we walked to the corner store to buy a bottle of pop, the owner was Black, and the people standing in front of and behind us in line were too. Many Black businesses were sprinkled throughout the neighborhood: cleaners, dentists' and doctors' offices, stores, insurance and tax representatives, record shops, car dealerships, restaurants, beauty salons, newspapers, nonprofit agencies, and art studios, just to name a few.

On a sunny day, our community parks were filled with throngs of Black residents. Occasionally there were special events held there. So many people from the neighborhood would attend, you couldn't find a place to park—it was a fantastic time! Not only that, but African American churches thrived. Blacks filled the pews in churches of all denominations and stripes. Almost every church had a full choir, and the community had an innate love and respect for God's house.

The most beautiful feature of our neighborhood during that time was a special relational connectivity—everybody knew everybody. Or, if they didn't know you, they knew a relative or someone else who did know you. This connectivity made it virtually impossible to drive down any street in our neighborhood and not know at least two or three families living on the block. Though our neighborhood had its issues, we were connected, and mutual love and respect were generally present. This camaraderie gave us all a strong sense of identity and belonging. We were proud to live in the North and Northeast Portland neighborhood.

Sorrowfully, those days are a memory. Only a faint sweet aroma lingers. African American businesses are now few and far between in the neighborhood. Many of our community-wide events have dismal African American presence. And we can now drive street after street without knowing a single soul who lives on any block. Gone, displaced, and moved are the majority of the African American people who once made up our beloved community.

In her article on dwindling diversity, Nikole Hannah-Jones writes, "Portland, already the whitest major city in the country, has become whiter at its core even as surrounding areas have grown more diverse." She goes on to say,

> The city core didn't become whiter simply because lots of white residents moved in, the data show. Nearly ten thousand people of color, mostly African Americans, also moved out. And those who left didn't move to nicer areas. Pushed out by gentrification, most settled on the city's eastern edges, according to the census data, where the sidewalks, grocery stores and parks grow sparse, and access to public transit is limited.[1]

Those ten thousand who have been pushed out by gentrification are people who once lived in our church's neighborhood. Statistically, our neighborhood, North and Northeast Portland, is where the largest population of Blacks historically have lived in Oregon, although in comparison to many other major cities, the overall Black population is small. But we are there no more.

Here's a historical snapshot of the peak and current decline of the African American population of my neighborhood. This data is from a study by the Portland Housing Bureau, utilizing 2010 US Census information.

> ➤ 1980 total population of Blacks in North/Northeast Portland was 22,387, equaling 28 percent.

> ➤ 1990 total population of Blacks in North/Northeast Portland was 23,724, equaling 31 percent.

> ➤ 2000 total population of Blacks in North/Northeast Portland was 19,922, equaling 25 percent.

> ➤ 2010 total population of Blacks in North/Northeast Portland was 12,274, equaling 15 percent.

In my estimation, our population numbers have declined even more since 2010. It will be interesting to see what the next wave of data shows. Now our church is the only building left on our block from yesterday—and the only place where longtime residents of yesterday's neighborhood gather.

On a painfully comical note, recently I came across a news clip that listed the ten "hippest" cities to live in the United States. It caught my curiosity, so I cruised through the list. To my amazement, the hippest city was Portland, Oregon. That by itself, however, was not the kicker. The kicker was that the picture the article used to show the hotspot in Portland was taken right across the street from our church—I could see it out of my office window. I thought to myself, "Wow, what was once the Hood is now a national Hipsterville!"

MOVED PRICES

Living in "Hipsterville" is expensive, and the movement in the cost of living is one reason why many long-term members of our community have been pushed out. Most people simply cannot afford to live in their old neighborhood anymore. Rents and mortgages cost too much, and there are numerous factors that figure into this unjust equation. To assume the price hikes are just the result of the progression of time is naive. Historical practices such as red-lining, city policies and planning, employment disadvantages, lack of quality educational opportunities, and racism are all, to some degree, culprits. All these factors contribute to why people with dollars are moving in and people without dollars are moving out.

In 1996, our church paid $365,000 for our current building. Today that same property is worth multiple millions of dollars. Currently, there is a fourteen-unit luxury environmental living complex being built a half block from our church called the Carbon 12. The price range for the units is $730,000 to $1.55 million. Directly opposite of our church parking lot and across the street are complexes that cost tens of millions of dollars to build—so you can imagine how high the rent is. If someone's income is far below the median level, it's impossible to live in an apartment where rent is between $1,500 and $2,800 a month, or to buy a house where the average price is $500,000. Truly, someone has moved our church's neighborhood.

A BIGGER ISSUE

Though our church is racially diverse, our dilemma centers around the gentrification of an African American neighborhood. The issue of moved neighborhoods is not exclusively a Black neighborhood problem, though! I've been around the block enough times to know that in many instances, when race is mentioned, people either tune in or tune out. Please resist the temptation to disengage.

Churches in other diverse contexts are experiencing moving neighborhoods. And from a biblical standpoint we understand Jesus is equally concerned about each neighborhood! All we have to do is follow the footsteps of Jesus into the various cities he ministered in to see his love and concern for their communities. For example, he had to go through a racially divided Samaria to pour out his love on the city of Sychar (Jn 4). And in an expression of deep, compassionate motherly love, he wept over Jerusalem saying that he longed to gather them as a hen gathers her chicks under her wings (Mt 23:37). Jesus' heart hasn't changed: your neighborhood still has an affectionate place in his heart!

And Jesus desires for his church to faithfully fulfill the call he has entrusted to them—even in a changing environment.

In 2017, *USA Today* did a piece titled, "Houses of Worship Do Some Soul-Searching as Their Neighborhoods Change."[2] The article discusses how churches all over the nation are facing the challenging of surviving in rapidly changing or changed neighborhoods. It highlights the fact that this phenomenon is not exclusive to African American neighborhoods but applies to others as well. Churches everywhere are getting caught in the quagmire of neighborhood transition. Whether the cause is gentrification, congregational aging, redevelopment projects, or a cultural swing, churches are left unable to grab the rope. The truth of the matter is, if your church is going to navigate your new neighborhood, it will have to walk through a healing process and do some hard work on multiple levels.

Has your church's neighborhood moved? Is your church now part of a new or a different neighborhood? Is your neighborhood experiencing a metamorphosis? If your answer to these questions is yes, the next chapter will help you better understand the impact of what has happened to you and your church. You will discover you have suffered something you may not have expected.

CHAPTER 2

DISCOVERING THE
HEALING PROCESS

It goes without saying that it would be difficult for any church to navigate a new neighborhood if it is knocked out, lying face-down on the canvas. It's also highly improbable that a church will immediately leap back on its feet after suffering the devastating blow of neighborhood displacement. Recovery is a process requiring time. Time to work through the pain. Time to clear the visional fog. Time to recalibrate the missional nerves and muscles. Time to receive healing and wholeness. And time to regain the relational balance needed for the church to minister to the neighborhood. First, we have to understand the process, and then we have to walk through it.

This process involves the seasons or phases a church experiences and must work through in order to recover from loss. Sure, it would be nice if God miraculously healed our pain and immediately restored what has been removed. However, he chooses to walk us though the valley and not transport us out of it. As with any type of significant loss, dealing and coping with a church's grief takes time and work. In *A Grief Observed*, C. S. Lewis journals about his personal discovery concerning grief. He writes, "The other end I had in view turns out to have been based on a misunderstanding. I thought I could describe a state; make a map of sorrow. Sorrow, however, turns out to be not a state but a process."[1]

Lewis's words not only ring true on a personal level but also chime powerfully in the soul of a church trying to regain its equilibrium. In Lewis's terms, to clear up any "misunderstanding," we must understand that getting our missional, visional, and relational feet back under us does not have a simple canned solution. It's not a state with calculated dimensions and a handy road map. It is a process where journeying will be required.

Our church's experience in identifying a healing process was arduous. Honestly, we were pretty clueless, and for years we failed to even recognize that we needed a healing process. For us, one of the early indicators that neighborhood change was occurring was a shift in our community conversation. Typically, when things were "normal," the conversations around our neighborhood were about people, places, and projects we were all aware of. Over time, however, different questions began to fill up the communication channels: What happened to this or that business? Where is this family or that family? Who is building that new structure? Where are all these White people coming from?

The problem wasn't so much that these changes were occurring but that our community was not being included in this new neighborhood narrative. I remember numerous conversations with church members and longtime neighborhood residents that could be categorized under the caption, "What in the world is going on?!" We were dazed, frustrated, and angry. We were wondering where in the world God was in all this transitional sludge. We prayed for a canned solution and a quick fix for our dilemma.

But, like Lewis, we had to discover that God's answer was for us to learn and walk through the process.

The difficulty in understanding and identifying the need for a healing process is rooted in our inability to sort out the confusing internal web tangled within our souls and minds. We are so busy trying to make sense of the overwhelming external reality that we overlook what is happening to us internally. We are so preoccupied with what is developing on the ground level that we fail to give the needed attention to what is being deconstructed beneath us, within our hearts. In other words, we do exactly what God says humans do: we look at the outward appearance of things and not so much at the heart (1 Sam 16:7).

When we suffer personal loss, we can walk into a pastor's or counselor's office and find help to get through our pain and hardships. But who tells the church how to cope with the loss of a neighborhood and how to recognize and walk through a necessary healing path or process? Who explains to the church why understanding this process is important and describes exactly what it looks like?

Thankfully, our church was eventually able to identify our process—though only after we had journeyed through it for several years. However, after we were able to wrap our minds and hearts around it, our church found a great source of comfort, healing, and encouragement.

Over the last few years, I've had the opportunity to share this process with a few churches and their leadership teams. To my surprise, their responses were all very similar. First, they all were comforted to discover a framework that articulated what they were feeling and experiencing. Second, they were given the freedom to mourn and weep and express their pain. Finally, they were energized to reengage their new neighborhood in faithful ministry. Here's what we've learned. Hopefully it will be of help to you too.

UNFOLDING THE PROCESS

To begin, I will outline the process, and then I will unpack it in the following chapters. The process consists of seven phases a church experiences and has to work its way through in order to recover and navigate its old but new neighborhood. See table 1 for a simple overview diagram showing each of the phases.

Table 1. Phases to work through in order to recover and navigate your old but new neighborhood

The Process	
Regular	*The process of remembering your old neighborhood*
Recognition	*The gradual awareness of your moving neighborhood*
Realization	*The realization of your moved neighborhood*
Reconstruction	*The attempt to rebuild your moved neighborhood*
Rage	*The anger over your moved neighborhood*
Reconciliation	*The coming to terms with your moved neighborhood*
Revamp	*The navigation of your church in a new neighborhood*

The first three phases—regular, recognition, and realization—occur prior to the finality of a moved neighborhood. However, they are still very real parts of the process simply because churches need to understand how they have emotionally arrived at the place where they are presently. A neighborhood move is not an overnight process, and even though a church may have been subtly aware of what was taking place, the whole time there was dismantling taking place in its soul. This dismantling produces questions—and a sense of helplessness and pain that must be addressed in order for a church to find healing and new strength. The next three phases—reconstruction, rage, and reconciliation—are equally important. Reconstruction deals with the church's attempts to transform the neighborhood back into what it once was. Rage addresses the deep anger the church feels because of what has occurred. And reconciliation is the process of the church coming to grips with its new reality in order to move forward. These phases are the essential steppingstones that empower the church to reach the revamp phase, where the church can grapple with the hard questions it must answer to refuel its mission and vision for its future. Each community will navigate these seasons differently and on different timetables. However, moving through each stage is critical for a congregation's long-term healing and resilience.

Let's begin unfolding the healing process by looking backward to the time when our neighborhood was normal.

CHAPTER 3

REGULAR

The *regular* component of the process embraces the adage "home sweet home." In the hearts of the long-term members of our communities, there exists the reality of how the neighborhood used to be—what it was like when the Hood was "regular." Vivid in their hearts and imaginations are the aromas of neighborhood barbecues. The joy of walking their children to their first day of school. Worshiping on Sundays in a community they know like the back of their hand. Eating in little cafes where they know the owners and cooks on a first name basis. Sitting on the porch and talking to people they have known for years. And frequenting all the neighborhood spots they affectionately refer to as "ours." Of course, they also remember the struggles and difficulties. However, woven into the memories of the difficulties is a strand of sweetness that comes from knowing *we* faced *our* problems together. The sum total of the old neighborhood, all the good and the bad, equates to one thing in their hearts and minds—home sweet home!

When thinking about when things were regular in our neighborhoods, there may be a real temptation to say, "Forget the past and move on. Those days are gone forever, so just get over it!" But whoa! Hold on for a second. Put on the brakes and resist that temptation. While there is an inherent wisdom in many situations about letting go of the past and moving on, this is not one of them. There is a cathartic element in acknowledging and remembering what was once dear to us. And it is a necessary part of the process to help move our churches to a new place where they can once again missionally engage in God's purposes and plan for the community.

THE IMPORTANCE OF REMEMBERING

There are two critical reasons why the regular stage is an important part of the process.

The first reason is identity. Many factors contribute to the formation of our identities—our upbringing, our faith, our education, and so forth. Our neighborhood and community are also on this list. We grow and form in the rich soil of our neighborhoods— we are "homegrown." When we meet someone for the first time, often one of the first things we learn about them is where they are from. Knowing where someone is from gives us a little sliver of information about who they are. Our neighborhood and community don't comprise the totality of who we are, but they do contribute to the formation of our identity.

When a neighborhood is displaced, so is a piece of our collective identity. That's why it creates a kind of "culture shock." When people are in a totally foreign environment, they can lose their bearings and sense of identity. They long for home sweet home and face the arduous challenge of reorienting themselves in strange land. This culture shock is one reason why the regular phase is important. Leaders need to help these long-term residents restore the parts of their identity that have been shaken. This is imperative because identity is crucial to mental wholeness, mission, and ministry.

There was a time when I literally knew almost everyone in our community. When my son was younger, we would go to the store or the park and almost every person we passed by would say, "Hey Mark, how's it going?" My son would ask, "Dad, how come you know everyone, and they know you?" My answer was, "Son, I have been around here a long time." Those relationships help to forge my identity and relationship to my community. Now I can walk by fifty people and I don't know any of them, and they don't know me. That messes with my sense of identity because I felt called by God to pastor a community I knew. But where is that community now? This created in me a bit of identity chaos. It made me wonder, *Who am I?*

Validation is the second reason why acknowledging the regular stage is important. When a neighborhood is displaced, the press often applauds the new neighborhood while sometimes unknowingly giving a "thumbs down" to the old neighborhood. The notion that the new is so much better than what was is a hard pill to swallow for long-term residents. It feels like a lack of acknowledgment that anything of meaning existed before the new neighborhood moved in.

One day I was standing in our church parking lot, and I noticed a group of about twenty-five people walking down the block with two guys leading them. I happened to know one of the guys in the group, and he yelled out to me, "Mark, come over here for a second." So I walked across the street and joined the group for a minute. They were on a guided tour of the neighborhood, and they were learning about all the new buildings, businesses, restaurants, and so on. So, the guy who called me over asked the guide if I could talk about the neighborhood for a minute. He told the group, "Hey everybody, this is Pastor Mark. He has been here in this neighborhood forever." So I obliged and told the group what the neighborhood used to be like. I explained that the place where the giant apartment complex now stands used to be a hub of neighborhood activity, where you could find the Golden House of Styles, Willie's Barbershop, the House of Sounds, and Doris' Cafe—all thriving community businesses. I told them that where the new organic grocery store now sits was once the bread factory. As I talked, the group became more intrigued. However, I noticed the guides were becoming a bit perturbed because I focused on what *was* and not simply on what *is*. So I quit my commentary. In their minds, what *was* had no value. They were a couple of young hipsters, and from the look on their faces, I could tell my brief history lesson didn't score too high on their interest chart. I was a bit saddened when I left the group. Unfortunately, people who remain in our neighborhood have had to swallow a lot of this kind of devaluation, and it is not too tasty. By revisiting the regular phase, the negative impact on our identity and our esteem emerges.

MOVING THROUGH REGULAR

To address the importance of the regular phase in our church, we've worked to provide space to reminisce. And we've worked to show our community that we still have our identity even though the ethos, demographics, and topography of our community have changed. We want them to know that even if the landmarks are gone, the good values we had as a community are still present within us.

By creating space, we give people permission to reminisce about their old neighborhood and feel good about it. I equate it to putting them in a room with an old dear friend they haven't seen in a long time. It's amazing to watch. Their eyes light up and smiles beam across their faces. The chatter is lively, and laughter fills the room. We have created these spaces in breakout sessions during our larger gatherings, personal conversations, and strategic discussion times during workshops or other events. I'm always for simplicity. So identify what in your context works best to bring people together for informal and open conversation— perhaps a small group in someone's home, or a Bible study night, or even a special gathering. The goal is to let people freely talk about the neighborhood they dearly miss.

In this simple process, amazingness happens. Incredible positivity and healing emerge in the hearts of the people. Sometimes people come away with life-giving statements that refuel the esteem and value that has ebbed away. After one workshop where we had talked about our regular, one woman spoke out to the group with a huge grin stretched across her face: "We had a great neighborhood!" Her statement was organic and uncontrived, and it brought life and joy to the room. And you could see others nodding their heads and saying along with her, "Our neighborhood was pretty awesome!" These kinds of statements reach deep into the souls of those who are now foreigners in their own neighborhoods. Such simple words can help liberate their souls from the adverse psychological messaging associated with the new neighborhood. By God's grace, they begin to bring healing from the blow that was dealt.

Another church, after talking about their regular, came up with a creative idea to acknowledge the old neighborhood and affirm the long-term residents in their community. They realized that much of the local history of their neighborhood was unknown and would simply die because people were unaware of their regular. So they developed a cool book that contained information about people, places, and events in the old neighborhood. They highlighted the popular places people frequented. They talked about some of the heroes of the community and the contributions they made to make the neighborhood a better place. They talked about some of the events that joined them together as a community. It was impossible to wade through the pages of the book and not feel good about what their neighborhood used to be. The added benefit is that, through the book, others have a chance to visit the old neighborhood. Similarly, when we lead our community through this phase of the process, God may give us some unexpected, wonderful ideas and gifts that foster healing and affirmation.

NAVIGATING THE MOVE

Let me offer three suggestions to help facilitate conversation in the space you provide for remembering and celebrating the regular phase.

First, frame the conversation. Dealing with the issue of a moved neighborhood is a heavy and weighty topic. Therefore, it is easy for lament to surface and arise to the forefront of the conversation. But this is not the goal of these conversations. Your aim is to produce a "sweet conversation," not a bitter one. You may start by saying something like, "We are going to have some fun together today. We are all going to take a Sunday stroll down memory lane and talk about our old neighborhood. We are going to talk about the good things we remember about our community. Are you ready for some sweet reminiscing? Then let's do it!" Or if you have an idea that's way better than this suggestion, feel free to go for it. What's important is that you set the parameters for the conversation in order to set the right tone.

Second, use strategic conversation starters and questions. To help facilitate and guide the conversation, the following prompts work well:

> Remember when our neighborhood was . . .

> What I liked the most about our neighborhood was . . .

> Where were the best places to eat in our neighborhood?

> Who was the one person you admired the most?

➤ In what ways did we care for each other in our neighborhood?

➤ What were the good values we had as a neighborhood?

Third, conclude by affirming the conversation: "We had a great time tonight sharing our stories and memories." Thank people for sharing. Remind them that they still carry what's valuable from the old neighborhood and that God still has a plan even though things are drastically different. Yes, there is more work to do, but this piece is needful, so embrace it.

Moving on from regular, the next phase of the process is recognition. Recognition is a phase that is easily missed because it is often unrecognizable. But in the next chapter we will make it clear and discover what happens when we recognize that change is indeed taking place in our neighborhood.

CHAPTER 4

RECOGNITION

I was heading to a lunch appointment at a new Thai restaurant about a mile or so away from our church. Driving to the restaurant was a cinch. Make a right on Williams and a left on Skidmore and, depending on traffic, you're there in about four minutes. I've driven and walked that route hundreds of times in the last forty years. When I was a kid, one of my best friends lived on Skidmore, and we played so much basketball, baseball, and every other ball on that street that I should have been a pro! During my later teenage years, our house was on the corner of Williams. The church parsonage where my wife and I first lived was on Skidmore, just three blocks west of Williams. The restaurant I was heading to was a straight four-block shot from our old house. So I had no need for any type of GPS assistance—I could get there with my eyes closed. Right?

Wrong! While creeping along in slow traffic—which in times past was never a problem—I began panicking. I couldn't find Skidmore Street! I thought to myself, *Mark, you're tripping or having some type of mental episode here. Where in the world are you? Where is Skidmore*

Street? It was no joke! I was disoriented—absolutely lost. So, telling myself to relax, I took a deep breath, and my bearings slowly started to return. My sense of direction recalibrated, and I realized I had driven a few blocks past Skidmore. Relief set in and the panic subsided, but I was still a bit puzzled.

Don't get me wrong. Everybody misses making a turn every now and then. But this was different. In an attempt to figure out what had just happened, I conducted a kind of self-evaluation test. I circled around a few blocks and drove the Williams to Skidmore route once again. When I made it to the corner of Williams and Skidmore, I said to myself, *Really, this is Skidmore and Williams?* It was astonishing. Every landmark that was once there was gone—vanished! The one-story Oregon Association of Minority Entrepreneurs building that stretched an entire block was gone. The same building where for years my uncle had his barbecue restaurant—gone! Only the Lord knows how many ribs I had eaten sitting on that corner. Now in its place was a massive five-story apartment complex with offices and shops on the lower level. On the other side of the street, Geneva's Social Club once stood. But the once most famous social club in Northeast Portland—along with the large grass field next to it—gone! In its place was a massive apartment building with restaurants, shops, and business spaces. And the parking lot on the adjacent corner next to the historic AME Zion Church—gone! For years, I had walked and driven past that lot and had seen a white El Camino parked in the same spot every day. But now there was a large apartment complex with restaurants, a donut shop, and a myriad of other shops. And Dansby's automotive garage building with the fancy sign—the garage where my little brother worked on cars for a spell—was also gone.

In that instant, I had a heartbreaking epiphany. My innate roadmap, etched by years of charting, had become a relic—outdated and unreliable. The neighborhood my heart knew internally was no longer an external reality. The neighborhood I'd once known no longer existed. It had been moved! Yes, the old buildings and landmarks were gone. But what cut deeper and was far more painful to accept was that the people were gone too.

WAKING UP TO THE CHANGE

The *recognition* phase of the process is when you start to notice or gain awareness that your neighborhood is slowly moving. Subtly, the demographics, the narrative, and the economics are shifting. In many instances the changes are not glaring enough to alarm you, but they are enough for you to raise an eyebrow and ask, "What is that?"

I have heard people in neighborhoods that have been displaced say, "I knew something was happening. I saw some changes, but I didn't realize what was going on until it was too late." It's kind of like speeding through a small town where, by the time you blink, you are out of there. However, though the recognition phase moves swiftly, there are some opportunities for the church. It can either be proactive and progressive or doze off and become inactive.

Sadly, as a leader in our community, I succumbed to the wrong possibility during the recognition phase. Even though I saw the way the neighborhood was changing, I was drowsy and did not wake up in time to avert some of the harmful changes. My response was like a nap I once took. It was around dinnertime and I was snoozing away. I was exhausted. I was snoring but I was still aware of what was going on in my house. I could smell the aroma of the food on the stove. I could hear my girls talking in their room. And I heard my wife calling me downstairs to eat my dinner. But the problem was I couldn't move. My mind was telling me to go eat, but I couldn't shake the sleep. Finally, I heard my wife tell our youngest son to go upstairs, wake up me up, and tell me to come eat. I heard their whole conversation, and I knew in a matter of seconds he would be coming into the room to wake me. But was I up to greet him? No! So Myles, my son, came into the room, positioned himself three inches from my ear, and screamed, "Dad, it's time to eat!" In an instant I jumped out of the bed and attempted to grab him. But by the time I reached out, he had already bolted down the stairs, laughing as he flew.

THE FOUR FOGS

The point of my story is that even though we might recognize something is morphing in our neighborhoods, sometimes we are in a drowsy fog that prevents us from doing something about it.

First, there is the fog of ignorance, which causes us to not understand how these changes will ultimately affect our neighborhood. There is a failure to cognitively process that the small waves we are noticing are a precursor to the tidal wave that will wash away our beloved community. There is also ignorance about what to do about what is going on. Who do we talk to—city planners, politicians, the mayor? Where do we go to find help—the state capital, city hall, businesses?

This fog of ignorance leads into the second fog: powerlessness. This fog makes us feel as if we have no ability to make a difference or impact the situation. Many churches do not have the exorbitant resources and connections to combat the barrage of forces they are fighting against. In many cases, what is occurring is outside of the church's realm of expertise. So leaders may feel as if there is nothing they can do.

Third, there is the fog of preoccupation. Most church leaders have a smorgasbord of projects on their plate and don't have the bandwidth to deal with another issue. There is simply too much other pressing stuff to deal with.

Fourth, there is the fog of tiredness. We just don't have the physical and mental energy it takes to deal with such a mammoth issue. We are overworked. In some cases we're stressing out to make ends meet on a church and personal level. The candle is burnt on both ends, and it is a lights-out situation. It's not that we don't care, but we are simply tired and depleted of our strength.

Sadly, in many communities, once the fog lifts we find our neighborhoods are bulldozed away. And we hadn't even put up a fight because we were drowsy and inactive during our recognition phase.

A CLEARING IN THE FOG: STRATEGIC ACTION

The other way we can respond when we recognize our neighborhood is changing is with strategic action. I wish I had known this several years ago. Generally, there are a few forces that move neighborhoods. The culprits are public policy—meaning zoning and development procurements—and economic factors such as banking and predatory practices, property development, and affordable housing. The negative neighborhood effect of these forces can be summed up by one truth: if people can't afford to live in a certain place, they will move to a place they can afford. And when the people are gone, so is the neighborhood. One strategy some neighborhoods have used successfully is community organizing. Community organizing and development is a process by which a community empowers itself by working to identify its needs and to resolve its problems in a collective manner. This grassroots process allows individuals and organizations to come together and join forces to speak up, influence policies, and create options to keep their neighborhoods intact.

One great example of the power of community organizing is taking place in Jackson Heights in Queens, New York, through a group called Chhaya that is working with people of South Asian and Indo-Caribbean origin. Jackson Heights has a rich history of being one of the most racially diverse areas in the country. However, for years they have combated forces that have sought to displace and move their neighborhood. Management companies have aggressively sought to displace tenants through unethical practices such as insane rent increases, ridiculous fees, neglected repairs, and perpetual harassment to drive tenants out of their apartments. Their goal is to change the neighborhood by moving in a higher income demographic. When they recognized these forces at work,

> local residents decided to fight back and reached out for support. To respond, Chhaya's organizers worked with other community-based organizations in Queens to organize tenants, homeowners, and local businesses. We organized in dozens of buildings to create multilingual, multi-ethnic building associations in order to grow the leadership of tenants, conducted know-your-rights workshops, and took group legal recourse against management companies when necessary. This work was done in six languages, and Chhaya built the model from scratch. Though it took a great deal of time and resources to develop, we were able to preserve thousands of units across the city with our coalition partners. This strategy resembles the grassroots efforts of dozens of local organizations in National CAPACD's network, working tirelessly to preserve the neighborhoods that these communities call home.[1]

Another example of the power of community organization comes from the Bay area, where there are literally more vacant homes than there are people homeless. So four mothers who were struggling to find a place to live organized themselves as Moms 4 Housing. Taking matters into their own hands, they moved into a house in West Oakland that had been vacant for two years. They ended up being violently evicted by police, but something wonderful happened as a result. They received great community support as well as overwhelming support from the media, and they earned the right to housing. Not only that but they inspired a strategy to fight gentrification, displacement, and unfair housing policies. They have spurred on the involvement of land trusts to purchase vacant properties and to make them affordable for low-income residents. Also, they make their voice heard on policy issues and planning.[2] These women recognized what was going in their neighborhood and they acted.

Regardless of how you responded during the recognition phase—whether you were groggy like I was or proactive like the organizers mentioned here—I offer you some pastoral wisdom here. First, if you are kicking yourself for what you didn't do—stop it. God's grace is sufficient for you, and you are still in the game. God is not finished using you yet. Use your God-given energy for changing your neighborhood today and tomorrow. Don't waste it on yesterday's mistakes. Second, even if you did respond proactively, you probably still did not change everything you wanted to. Don't be discouraged. Celebrate your victories and keep up the good work—you have and are making a difference!

NAVIGATING THE MOVE

In navigating the recognition phase, placing yourself somewhere you can be observant is important. Here are a few suggestions that may be helpful.

Slow down. Sometimes our pace is so fast we miss out on what is going on in our surroundings until it's too late. Personally, I was busy trying to take care of our congregation, raise money to build the church, and attend to the host of other community endeavors I was involved in. My fast pace contributed to my missing the obvious. I'm sure I'm not the only one guilty of breaking the ministry speed limit, but that still is no excuse to keep the pedal to the metal. We have to slow down so we can observe what is happening in the environment around us. Making sure we have a sabbath day to rest is a great place to start. Then learning how to take and schedule pitstops during our daily routine and week will help as well. Ready, set, stop—or rather, slow down!

Take inventory. Keep a running list of the elements of your neighborhood that are changing around you. Once you realize too many things are missing, it will be like a splash of cold water waking you up out of a fog. Taking inventory helps you not to see these changes in isolation from each other. Keeping at least a mental inventory of your community will help you recognize the big picture of what is happening around you. For example, you recognize it is not one business that is missing; it is three or four that are gone. It's not just one family that has moved, but several are no longer living in the area. Get the picture—taking inventory will make sure that we do!

Engage in the right places. Hindsight is twenty-twenty. If all of us pastors who are lamenting over our gentrified neighborhoods had been at the table where zoning and policy were being crafted, we may have been able to stop the train from leaving the station—or at least keep the engine from leaving with so many cars. To aid in recognition, find gatherings that make decisions that affect your community—perhaps neighborhood meetings, city council meetings, or chamber of commerce meetings. Being in the right space helps you to recognize the changes that are coming before they happen and enables you to object or make other recommendations.

Self-recognition. It is critical that you understand that you are still present in your neighborhood for a divine reason. God has a plan, and you and your church are part of it. God has an answer, and you are a part of it. We will say much more about this in the following chapters, but for now, know that although massive changes have occurred in your neighborhood, God is not finished with you. Recognize that you are not just a victim but a vital instrument in God's hand who he will work through to bless your community.

Recognizing is one thing, but realizing what has actually happened to a church in a moved neighborhood carries even a bigger punch.

CHAPTER 5

REALIZATION

The 1965 World Boxing Council (WBC) championship bout between Muhammad Ali and Sonny Liston is one of the most controversial fights in boxing history. The fight was essentially over before it began. Early in the first round, Liston threw a left jab. Ali dodged it and threw a right jab so fast no one even saw the punch, making it one of the most infamous and debated jabs ever in boxing, dubbed the "phantom punch." Feeling the impact of the blow, Liston fell to the canvas and was unable to get back up on his feet. In two minutes and twelve seconds the fight was over. Ali won; Liston lost!

Captured in that moment was one of the most recognized photos in sports history. In the picture, Ali is postured in a gladiator stance, with every muscle in his body taunt and rippling. His sculpted arm is extended in an upward trajectory across his chest with his fist tightly clenched. On his face is the grimace of a lion that has captured its prey. At his feet, lying beneath on the canvas, is Liston—hurt, broken, and unable to stand, the unfortunate victim of that traumatic phantom punch.

When a church's neighborhood is moved, it experiences a traumatic blow, the impact of which has the potential to buckle its soul and send it reeling down onto a harsh canvas. Though at times it is thrown with lightning speed, and spectators may fail to see it hit or understand the adverse impact, the blow is nonetheless real. The church feels it. And its effects are painfully devastating and, in some instances, debilitating.

WE REFUSE TO SING

Psalm 137:1-4 exposes the deep trauma of a people hit by a brutal blow of displacement. The psalm amplifies the lament of Jews who had been taken captive from their homeland during the seventy-year Babylonian exile.

> By the rivers of Babylon
>   we sat and wept
>   when we remembered Zion.
> There on the poplars
>   we hung our harps,
> for there our captors
>   asked us for songs,
> our tormentors demanded songs of joy; they said,
>   "Sing us one of the songs of Zion!"
> How can we sing the songs of the LORD
>   while in a foreign land?
>   (Ps 137:1-4 NIV)

This brief lament highlights the importance of place. The first place mentioned—Babylon—is shrouded in a cloak of pain. But the other—Zion—is referenced with heartfelt affection and longing.

Babylon is the land of their captivity. It is a place of pain. Even though the prophet Jeremiah commanded them to engage in city life and seek the Lord's blessing in the land of their exile (Jer 29:7), this was difficult for them to do. Babylon was not their home! It was a foreign environment void of their history, their community, and the nuances of the everyday life they once knew. Knowing fully that their displacement was a result of their disobedience— and knowing it was God's sovereign will that permitted the Babylonian military to execute judgment—did not lessen the traumatic blow of displacement. They felt lost in their new surroundings. Hence, they called it a "foreign land," or as translated in the King James Version, a "strange land." It was a strange place they neither loved nor wanted to be in.

At the other end of the spectrum is the place called Zion. For the exiles, Zion is home sweet home. Zion was an integral part of their community identity, their existence, and a major shaping force in their communal and personal understanding of God. Their affectionate disposition toward their beloved Zion is expressed in their sorrowful reaction when they reminisce over the city. Psalm 137:1 tells us that when they remembered Zion, they sat and wept for a place that for them was no more. Their homesick souls buckled and fell to the canvas.

In Zion, they could sing. Within the context of their own culture and community life, they could belt out heartfelt songs reverberating with melodious joy. In Zion they could sing songs with robust theological meaning about a God who had blessed their lives and their place. But now that the place of their song was gone, their music ceased. Their harps, which were once held in their hands, now hung silently on the branches of the poplar trees. Victims of displacement, their tongues had become mute, and their skilled fingers had stopped strumming. How could they sing in a place that was not their own? They longed for what used to be theirs—Zion!

In addition to the emphasis on place, the psalm reveals two other traumatic aspects of displacement. One, as briefly mentioned already, is the emotional impact displacement has on a people. The use of words such as *weep* and *tormentors* and the inability to sing songs of joy clearly show that displacement has the power to cut out the collective heart and emotional soul of a people. When a people lose their heart and soul, their movement comes to a halt. They experience a death of sorts. Life for the displaced is no longer "business as usual" because circumstances are not "as usual" anymore. It's as though their vital, life-giving oxygen is in short supply, and their only recourse is to sit and weep until they can recover.

The idea that they should just rise up and get over it is a farce. The blow was too severe for a quick "microwave" recovery. It will take time for them to navigate the rough healing terrain from displacement to wholeness. Even if they are able to integrate aspects of their previous life into Babylonian culture, they will never be able to transform Babylon into Zion. But they'll have to figure out how they can recover emotionally and one day sing again—even in Babylon! But the blow of displacement punishes more than just emotions. It also rattles purpose and mission.

Displacement can skew a people's purpose and mission. Going back to the psalm, those who refused to sing were minstrels—professional musicians. They were individuals whose calling in life was to worship and praise God, to lift and educate the minds and spirits of others through the ministry of music. Think of the many hours, days, months, and years of study they may have logged honing their skills. Now, after experiencing a harsh blow, their core mission and purpose in life were knocked out—lying on a Babylonian canvas, or rather hanging on a tree!

Due to the change of place and the difficulties that accompanied it, they saw no context for their life's mission and purpose where they were now living. They saw God only as the God of their old neighborhood and not their new one. Their once vivid and bright purpose was now dark and obscure. In their view, God was not where they *are*—he was only present where they *were*. Perhaps they failed to see that even in their distress, God was equally present in their new environment, and God may have wanted their tormentors to hear the songs of Zion so that they could find freedom in the place where they live. Maybe the musicians missed a missional opportunity?

EMMANUEL CHURCH

One day I was having a conversation with Bishop C. T. Wells, pastor of Emmanuel Church. For decades Emmanuel Church has been a bright beacon in the North and Northeast neighborhood of Portland. It has always been on the cutting edge of developing and initiating new ministries to extend the kingdom of God and serve the community. It spearheaded and led community development projects and programs to serve those who are marginalized. Alongside the church's social arm of the ministry is its unwavering commitment to clearly communicate the gospel of Jesus Christ. Emmanuel Church has offered an exemplary model both for preaching to win people's souls and for reaching out to meet people's needs.

During our conversation, I asked Bishop Wells this question: "Has the removal of your neighborhood affected your church?" His lightning-quick response was an emphatic *yes*. I then asked if the impact of the neighborhood shift was positive or negative. Without hesitation, he responded, "Definitely negative!" He then went on to explain why he believed this was the case.

As he spoke, I could hear the tone of a pastor who was passionate about the welfare of his congregation and deeply concerned about the future of his church. He started off talking about the worship-gathering dynamics of the church. Attendance-wise, the church was taking a huge hit on Sunday mornings and during their midweek activities. The problem was the dispersion of the congregation: "The people live all over the place now." The majority of those who at one time lived close to the church now live too far away to come. Some come very sporadically, and some have even stopped attending church altogether. Rising housing prices have forced them to move into more affordable areas, where there are few churches that culturally resonate with them, so they come to Emmanuel when they can. For others, the hurdles and inconveniences are too great, so they don't worship anywhere at all. Bishop Wells's biggest concern was not how many people were attending services but the challenges these dynamics present to forming a cohesive community of believers. In times past this was never a problem. The church had been the gorilla glue that bonded the community together. He lamented, "It's just difficult to form community when all the same people are seldom present."

Our conversation then turned to ministry and outreach. In short, he told me they had to shut down the majority of their outreach ministries because the new people living in the neighborhood had no need for those services. "Dr. Mark," he said to me, "we are absolutely going to have to rethink and retool our outreach strategy to this community because on a goods and services level, they don't need what we were providing—they already have it!" In the same breath, he said, "Things are just so different. I used to know everybody in the neighborhood, and people in the church knew everybody. But that's not the case anymore. I don't know who these people are, and they don't know me or the church. This is a challenging situation. And urban pastors got to figure this out quick because if we don't, many of our churches will be extinct."

Our chat concluded with Bishop Wells sharing a conversation he recently had with a guest pastor who spoke at his church. This particular leader speaks extensively throughout the United States to hundreds of pastors annually. Bishop Wells was explaining to the guest pastor the difficulties Emmanuel Church was facing in trying to survive in a moved neighborhood. The pastor's response took him aback: moving neighborhoods are occurring all over the nation. This trend is not happening in a silo. Pastors and churches across the country are in a panic trying to figure out what to do in order to survive changing neighborhoods. The guest pastor went on to say that the majority of these pastors are tired, confused, and on the verge of calling it quits! Their entire ministry paradigm has been scrambled.

Bishop Wells concluded our conversation with these words: "Dr. Strong, churches are feeling the impact of this phenomenon all over, and something has to change or else!"

I concur with Bishop Wells 100 percent—something has to change! But before we try to "fix" the problem—which is the initial go-to move for most of us pastors and leaders—we have to first realize we've indeed been hit. We've experienced a traumatic blow, a phantom punch, that can scramble our heads and knock us off our feet. And it hurts!

My goal in sharing Psalm 137 was not to bog you down with exilic history but to make an important point. Regardless of how displacement happens, it creates a distressing experience. So, whether you are displaced by being moved out, or you're displaced by others moving in, it is a blow that

> ➤ Leaves you lamenting the loss of a place you once loved,

> ➤ Evaporates the joy that once filled your heart in your old neighborhood,

> ➤ Creates an internal war about either rejecting or accepting your new place in life and ministry,

> ➤ Forces a decision for you to forgive or not to forgive your tormentors,

➤ Demands a reshaping of your corporate identity,

➤ Challenges your community cohesiveness and vitality,

➤ Makes you rethink mission, purpose, and methodology,

➤ Clouds the reality of God's presence and faithfulness to you in a changed environment,

➤ Causes pain on personal and corporate levels that previously was not present, and

➤ Leaves you wondering what you are to do next.

I don't presume that every pastor, leader, and church feels or responds the exact same way to the blow of a moved neighborhood. That's simply not the case. Even in other situations, different people grieve differently when experiencing loss. So there is no universal appropriate response or way to lament a moved neighborhood. The neighborhood blow that you and your church encountered may have affected you in manner not discussed in the chapter. And there is also a remote possibility that you weren't dealt a blow but were delivered a blessing by such a move. If that is the case—wonderful!

However, for those whose experience has been far less than favorable, I assure you that you have a brother who understands your present fight. I affirm the reality that if your neighborhood has been moved, you have experienced suffering on some level. Like we used to say in my old neighborhood when we resonate with another person's painful experience, "Brutha, Sista, I can feel ya!" I affirm—you've been hit. The blow is real and is no phantom punch.

After recognizing your neighborhood is changing, what happens next is like a splash of cold water in the face. The harsh reality crystallizes, and you realize your home is not moving—it has moved! This phase of the process is called *realization*.

When we genuinely realize our neighborhood has moved, it is a hard pill to swallow, even if we have been present throughout the whole process. In Lance Freeman's book *There Goes the 'Hood: Views of Gentrification from the Ground Up*, he tells the story of a woman named Samantha who realizes her neighborhood has changed.

> I remember when I noticed things were definitely changing. There used to be a time when you did not see whites on Myrtle Avenue after the sun went down. That was unheard of. But I remember after about five years after I moved back [this would make it around 1992] saw a white guy using an ATM on Myrtle Avenue after dark. And this was an ATM that wasn't even enclosed. And it was like he was comfortable, "I'm home." That's when I realized things had changed. So now they're making Myrtle Avenue look real nice. It looks like Park Slope. I'll give you another example. For the longest time there's an A&P right around the corner. But I usually went shopping outside of the neighborhood so that I could get fresh meat, fresh produce. Just in the past couple of years they have been totally modernizing the store. To the point you would hardly recognize the store. So my son and his friend went in there and asked the manager, "Why are you fixing up the store now all of a sudden." And they said, "Because more whites are moving into the area."[1]

In Samantha's brief epiphany, three pieces of evidence confirm that her neighborhood has moved. The first is the demographics. Three times she mentions the presence of Whites in her neighborhood. Although there is nothing wrong with that, it was not the previous norm. Second, she talks about the changing landscape. Her neighborhood doesn't look like it used to. She says it is starting to look really nice, like another part of the city. She concludes with how the quality of the store is improving. They've remodeled the building and are stocking better foods.

I don't believe that anyone is against neighborhood improvement. However, when the improvement excludes longtime residents, it hurts.

Nehemiah 1:1-4 offers insight into this painful reality:

> The words of Nehemiah the son of Hachaliah.
>
> It came to pass in the month of Chislev, in the twentieth year, as I was in Shushan the citadel, that Hanani one of my brethren came with men from Judah; and I asked them concerning the Jews who had escaped, who had survived the captivity, and concerning Jerusalem. And they said to me, "The survivors who are left from the captivity in the province are there in great distress and reproach. The wall of Jerusalem is also broken down, and its gates are burned with fire."
>
> So it was, when I heard these words, that I sat down and wept, and mourned for many days; I was fasting and praying before the God of heaven.

From these few verses, we can tell that Nehemiah has a heartfelt concern for his hometown and those who live there. That's why he asks the question in the first place. When his brothers inform him of all the trauma and devastation that has occurred, he encounters a blow, a reality punch that knocks the wind out of him and sends him reeling into a place of mourning and grief. He hears that the people are in great trouble and are living in disgrace, and that the walls of his beloved city, which perhaps at one time surrounded his family and friends' neighborhood, were destroyed. This proved to be a reality he couldn't bear. I'm sure in that moment Nehemiah felt things could never get better—he was devastated!

When we come to grips with the reality that our neighborhood has changed, we too can experience a sense of hopelessness and devastation. The brunt of the blow can knock us off our feet. So what do we do when reality hits? How can we deal with such an emotional moment? Nehemiah provides us some answers for how we can cope.

NAVIGATING THE MOVE

When Nehemiah was confronted with the realities in his community, he took several actions that we too can utilize to help us when we are working through our own process.

Nehemiah sat down. Sitting down is the act of getting off our feet so we can center and allow our thoughts, emotions, and physical responses to synchronize with each other. Sitting enables us to process all we are feeling and come to terms with our situation. Sitting also prohibits us from making knee-jerk reactions that may prove to be noneffective or even harmful.

So, on a practical note, if you find yourself in the reality phase, find a place where you can sit in quietness and be still without interruption.

Nehemiah mourned. He allowed himself to grieve the loss and devastation that occurred in his city. It is all right to grieve over our moved neighborhoods! It's okay to feel sad and broken over what has happened. Mourning is a holy and natural response to loss. And we have permission from the Scriptures to mourn over the loss we have experienced. Nehemiah mourned, and so can you and I.

Nehemiah wept. Tears are the liquid solvent that unburden the human soul. Nehemiah wept. Jeremiah wept. And Jesus wept. If we cry over our neighborhoods, we are in good company. So if our hearts are broken over what has happened, we don't need to hold back our tears. Our tears release God's grace into the depths of our soul, into the places where we need it most.

Nehemiah prayed and fasted. Though the reality of Jerusalem's situation was dire, Nehemiah prayed that God would work in the presence of crisis. We can pray similarly that God would work in our neighborhood even though we have suffered great loss. Coupled with his prayer was fasting. This was his way of expressing his earnestness to God. Fasting is a good discipline for us to incorporate with our prayers too.

Nehemiah placed himself before the God of heaven. Being before God is the key! Only God has the power to comfort our hearts in a way that makes sense. He alone has the power to lift our mind, emotions, and heart. Only he has the capacity to totally understand all the minutiae and nuances of how this reality is impacting us and those we love. He can fill us with hope when our reservoir is depleted. So being before him is of utmost importance. And the way we do this is by sitting, mourning, weeping, praying, and fasting. Though our neighborhood has moved, God hasn't! He is before us, so let us be before him!

CHAPTER 6

RECONSTRUCTION

"Humpty Dumpty sat on a wall, Humpty Dumpty had a great fall. All the king's horses and all the king's men couldn't put Humpty together again." Though juvenile, this old rhyme holds an element of truth: when something of value is lost or broken, our natural tendency is to attempt to repair it. We seek to put the pieces back together again. Once reality has set in and our community realizes it has lost something of great value, we turn our efforts to figuring out a way to make our neighborhood what it once was. We attempt to bring back a sense of normalcy to our altered world. Fueled with passion and a plethora of other emotions, the efforts are heartfelt and genuine. However, in many cases, the damage has been done and reversing it would be a feat of monumental proportions—and it is seldom accomplished. However, despite the unfavorable odds, we still try. In our community this phase played out in a number of ways.

TAKING BACK CONTROL

Throughout our community, we talked a lot about "taking back our neighborhood"—it was the resounding crescendo made by the voices of long-term residents. Whether in a barbershop, a grocery store, a church, or a restaurant, it was not uncommon to hear someone talking or asking about how we were going to get our neighborhood back. The feeling was, "We've got to do something about this!"

One of the five stages of grief is bargaining. Bargaining is a natural reaction to loss and feelings of vulnerability. The ultimate goal of the bargaining stage is for the individual who is suffering loss to gain a sense of control over the situation. These conversations that were occurring across our community were coming out of vulnerability and loss. They revealed a cry to change the neighborhood back to what it was and to regain a sense of control— even though it was impossible to turn back the hands of time. The conversations were to some degree cathartic. They gave people the motivation to change what they could and the opportunity to vent about what they couldn't.

As we attempted to reconstruct the neighborhood, we had a number of gatherings and meetings in churches and other community spaces to address policies, banking practices, the need for affordable housing, and so on. Since houses and properties were being bought up so rapidly by developers, these meetings were springing up every week. One meeting I remember was held at Vancouver Avenue Baptist Church. It was packed with people from the community. Blacks and Whites alike were crammed into the basement of the community landmark. Leading the discussion was Dr. Matt Hennessey. We spent a few hours talking about how we could restructure and prevent more removal of the neighborhood by preserving existing properties. Ideas surfaced about attempting to get certain neighborhood properties classified and protected as historical landmarks. Within the discussion that day, I distinctly remember hearing not only the words that were being spoken but the urgency, pain, and desperation in the voices of the neighborhood members.

Another meeting centered around retaining property and figuring out ways to curb taxes and access funds to prevent the remaining homeowners from losing their properties. We also discussed how we could keep some of our schools, which were the
pride and joy of the neighborhood, from going under due to lack
of funding and gentrification. These reconstruction meetings
were great, and some good work came out of them—some of
which is still going on today. However, in our case, the moving
trucks with our neighborhood loaded in the back were already
speeding down the highway at full speed. But that didn't stop the
efforts to try to reconstruct the neighborhood.

During the reconstruction phase of the process, we need to
resist the temptation to use our energy to be destructive. All the
pent-up rage can easily cause us to act out or vent in such a way
that our point is never heard. At some of the meetings some
people were so fired up that they did more harm than good. Sure,
they blew off a lot of steam and cleared their fire stack, but their
message missed the mark because their tone and actions were
totally destructive. Even though what they were saying was true,
influencers dismissed them and labeled them in a negative
manner. So in our desire to reconstruct, we need to use our energy
wisely—to think and discern what are the right battles for us to
fight. We should ask God for wisdom to fight them the right way,
and he will definitely help us. Though the reality is bleak and the
fight is uphill, we can still make a difference.

The nonprofit Africatown is a good example of a community
making positive inroads in reconstructing aspects of their moved
neighborhood. In Seattle, Washington, the Central District (CD)
was historically the primary hub for the African American population. But, like North and Northeast Portland, the CD has
become the epicenter of gentrification. The historical fingerprints
and footprints of the former residents have for the most part

vanished. In an attempt to preserve some of what was lost, K. Wyking Garrett and others formed an organization called Africatown. Africatown is a multifaceted organization that has formed a community-owned land trust to preserve and purchase properties, and worked with developers to build the Liberty Bank, which the community will own in fifteen years. Also in their plans for the near future is to build the African Village, which will give affordable housing options to remaining residents. Under the umbrella of Africatown are several organizations that focus on education, business development, technology, cultural preservation, and youth empowerment. The goal of all these is to empower, preserve, and reconstruct what they can of the moved Black neighborhood.

NAVIGATING THE MOVE

Let's revisit the Nehemiah story that we looked at in the last chapter, but this time through the lens of reconstruction. Remember that Nehemiah's grief was caused by the distress in Jerusalem due to the broken-down wall (Neh 1:1-4). The story was remarkable because God used a ragtag bunch to rebuild the wall in record time. I suspect that although they did in fact rebuild the wall, it did not look exactly like the one that had been destroyed. Different-shaped stones went into different places. The height in some spaces varied an inch or two, and the stones varied in their hues. My point is that, just like the Israelites could not build the exact same wall, neither can we reconstruct our neighborhoods into what they once were. There is going to be some difference, especially if the real estate is occupied by new buildings serving different purposes, and if the people who once filled those spaces are now gone. However, there are some that we can reconstruct that are of great value and can bring healing. There are some treasures we can use to reconstruct valuable elements of our old communities.

The treasure of prayer. Prayer is a treasure at our disposal to use for reconstruction, whatever that may look like. Nehemiah prayed to God throughout his story from start to finish. In other words, God's help was needed to start the rebuilding. God's help was needed to sustain them during the rebuilding. And God's help was needed for them to complete the rebuilding. Whatever we want to reconstruct, we will need God's help! The way to procure his aid is the same way Nehemiah and the Israelites did—through prayer. And when we pray, we need to pray for the big picture, for God's sustaining help through the process, and for the completion of something good and beneficial for our community.

Treasure of centering. The Quaker tradition practices what they call *centering*. Centering is a contemplative communion with God where the seeking soul can hear his voice and discover his will. Nehemiah engages in a centering of sorts (Neh 2:11-13). During the night he rides out in silence, not telling anyone where he is going or what God had placed in heart. That time for him was a space where he could see and listen to what God wanted to do in his city. As he quietly surveyed the city, he observed the cataclysmic crisis they were in. However, the voice of God quietly speaking spoke louder to his soul than the chaos of scattered rocks and an unprotected city. I encourage you to recognize that silence before God is an important treasure that has great value in reconstruction. The reality is that in order to *do*, we must *listen*. Centering helps us to listen so we can do.

The treasure of unity. Even though our community may be scattered, there are people who are still present. In Nehemiah's day, only a few exiles remained in Jerusalem. But the scarcity of population did not stop the rebuilding. A cohesive unity of those who remained formed to get the work done (Neh 3). It is so easy for us to focus on those who are gone and not see those who are left. But it is not those who are away who will get the work done;

it is those who are present. In Nehemiah 3 there is a simple phrase that is repeated over and over again: "next to." There is a diverse group of people working together—"next to" one another—ranging from perfume makers to farmers. Despite their differences they all worked in unity alongside each other. This unity is what it will take for us to reconstruct elements of our old neighborhoods. We can't do it by ourselves, nor can we make the difference with just our own church. Reconstruction will require us to work next to others who have the same heart, passion, and drive. Recently, a dozen or so pastors of churches in gentrified areas of Portland have begun to meet with one another. As a result of those meetings, we are being impacted, our churches are being helped, and we have plans to reconstruct aspects of the impacted community. Unity is a treasure.

The treasure of rubble. In Nehemiah 4:2, some adversaries taunt, "What are these feeble Jews doing? Will they fortify themselves? Will they offer sacrifices? Will they complete it in a day? Will they revive the stones from the heaps of rubbish—stones that are burned?" The answer to that last mocking question is yes! Isn't that how God works? He takes what is considered to be inadequate and uses it for his glory. Right now there are the fragments of our old neighborhoods laying in ashes at our feet. Heaps of rubbish and tons of displaced stones. Our tendency is to want to dismiss this debris and send it to the dump. Don't do it. Those remaining mounds of stone could be the very foundation God uses to reconstruct something beautiful in your community. Or to use a different comparison, Job 14:7-9 says,

> For there is hope for a tree,
> If it is cut down, that it will sprout again,
> And that its tender shoots will not cease.
> Though its root may grow old in the earth,

And its stump may die in the ground,
Yet at the scent of water it will bud
And bring forth branches like a plant.

So let's identify what we and God have to work with and forge a plan. Maybe God will send the scent of water and something miraculous will occur.

Even though we may not be able to make our neighborhood what it once was, we can still make a difference and let the new residents know we were and are here. That mission is possible despite the difficulties.

CHAPTER 7

RAGE

When our neighborhood moves, we experience anger—often the deep, brooding kind that is not easily appeased no matter how spiritual we are! This is real, life-altering anger that must be dealt with on both a personal level and a church-wide level. Think about it for a moment: how can we or our churches be missional if we are constantly ticked off at the people in our neighborhood? Understanding how to work through the *rage* phase is imperative.

This kind of rage is not going to be appeased by some simple slogan. It requires a deep work of God in our hearts—a work of the Spirit that lances the wound and flushes out the toxins so that new life can pour in. This work allows grace and mercy to sooth and repair the broken heart and replaces the fire of rage with the redemptive fire of the Lord Jesus Christ.

FOUR FIRE STARTERS

To work through our anger, it is important for us to understand the fire starters—the sparks that ignite our anger. The first is invasion. Gentrification is an invasion of a stranger into our space. And these strangers come not just to visit but to take over.

Consider for a moment if a stranger walked into your home, kicked off their shoes, and an hour later started throwing all your family mementos and heirlooms into the dumpster bin. How would you feel? I guarantee you would not be happy about it. And then, in addition, you find yourself powerless to put them out of your house or stop them from destroying what's dear to you. The unanticipated invasion of strangers in your neighborhood is a shock that fuels anger. There is a big difference between you welcoming someone into your home and someone else welcoming themselves into your home—not just to visit but to evict you and live in your home themselves!

Gentrification has occurred in almost every major metropolitan city in America, from Oakland, California, to Harlem, New York. However, Portland, Oregon, is the most gentrified city in the nation. In an article on gentrification, Mike Maciag writes: "A select group of cities experienced extensive gentrification in recent years. Perhaps nowhere were changes more visible than in Portland, where 58 percent of eligible tracts gentrified—more than any other city."[1]

A study done by Portland State University summarizes well the impact of what has happened in North and Northeast Portland. In addition, it addresses something called "root shock" that these neighborhoods experience when invaded.

> Housing is more than just shelter—it is part of a neighborhood, with access to amenities, services, and schools. But neighborhoods are more than just the opportunities in geographic proximity—they are communities that support families, social networks, religious, social, and cultural institutions. When neighborhoods and communities are disrupted

by redevelopment and market forces, there are real conse-
quences for the well-being of communities and the individuals they support. The impacts have been likened by re-
searcher Mindy Fullilove to "root shock"—as when a plant is
ripped from its soil, it may survive, but it does not fully recover as a robust organism. When people are displaced from
their emotional ecosystems, they are stressed, and communities falter. The experience of African-Americans in Portland
has been marked by several cycles of traumatic displacement—
from forced moves out of wartime worker housing to
Vanport; in the (un)natural disaster that was the Vanport
flood to the Albina district neighborhoods; and through the
construction of the Memorial Coliseum, I-5 and other
highway expansion projects, Legacy Emanuel Hospital's
planned expansion, and today by revitalization as a desig-
nated urban renewal area that fomented rapid gentrification.
Some have been displaced involuntarily by rising housing
prices; others have departed historically Black neighborhoods where they no longer feel at home.[2]

A few summers ago I was teaching a group of doctoral students
about the impact of gentrification on neighborhoods and the
church. During the break, a White pastor and I got into a conversation about what was happening in his town in California. His
church was 99.9 percent White, and their neighborhood had
changed. Many Hispanics and Blacks had moved into the area and
the church found itself in a crisis. His congregants were upset and
struggling because they did not feel at home anymore. He was
working through a quagmire of emotions trying to figure out
what in the world he was going to do.

Nothing in life remains the same forever, and all change is hard.
However, when our neighborhoods are invaded "by force," as the

study says, the root shock we experience will precipitate a response of anger.

Injustice is another spark that ignites anger. I attended a meeting where it was reported that one bank in our community had given out 104 loans in the span of a few years. Of those loans, four went to minorities and a hundred went to Whites. As I listened to the report, my jaw dropped. Just a few years earlier, my wife and I had applied for a home loan from that same bank. We definitely qualified, but they turned us down. Even our realtor, who was White, was furious because he thought there was no way we should have been denied. But we were, and I didn't find out why until years later when I attended this meeting.

Another form of injustice is lowballing people out of their property. So many people in our community basically had their property stolen from them. Developers would come in and buy prime property for nickels and dimes. I remember one family that was going to sell a piece of prime neighborhood property, and the developers offered them ten times less than what the property was worth. When you know these people and hear story after story of this kind of thing happening, the rage over the institutionalized policies that hurt the community and the greed of developers burn a hole in your soul, and you wish you could, like Jesus, turn over a few tables—and some other things too!

Insensitivity and ignorance are other sparks. When new businesses started popping up all over the neighborhood, a few ladies from our church decided to patronize a new ice cream shop across the street. Their intention was to splurge a bit and enjoy a cool treat on a hot day. Looking at the menu, they became outraged. One of the ice cream flavors on the menu was called "chocolate crack." Their anger was founded because of the damage the actual drug crack had done to members of our community. Crack cocaine had devastated our community! In fact, located right outside the door of the ice cream shop was a spot where much drug activity had occurred. During that time, very few families were not impacted by the crack epidemic in some way. Parents lost sons and daughters. Kids lost parents. Many users lost their dignity and respect, and some lost their lives.

The women were so upset they came to talk to the leadership of our church about what they saw on the menu at the ice cream shop. When I say they were hot—that would be an understatement. I listened to them and affirmed, comforted, and prayed with them, but that only brought the temperature of the fire down a few degrees. The women were mad enough to melt every container of ice cream in that shop! There was no way anyone who had any background understanding of the neighborhood would put an item on the menu called chocolate crack.

Northeast Community Church has been a part of the North and Northeast landscape of Portland for years. One day a well-meaning new neighborhood resident said to the pastor, "We are so glad you have come into our neighborhood—welcome!" The pastor then schooled him a bit, informing him that the church had been present in this location for over twenty-five years. The neighbor was trying to be hospitable, but his ignorance hit a raw nerve with the pastor. These micro-irritations caused by ignorance happen all the time. Insensitivity and ignorance in a moved neighborhood are commonplace. Most of the new residents have no reference point for the preexisting neighborhood. And often they lack the cultural competence to understand what is and what is not acceptable conversation or behavior. Sadly, many new people in the neighborhood are unaware of what they are saying and doing. And, in many cases, they are never in spaces or environments where they can discover their mishaps. This type of insensitivity happens so much it comes to be expected, but each time a long-term resident experiences it, it grates on their nerves and soul, fueling their anger.

Entitlement is also an anger igniter. Entitlement is the belief that one is inherently deserving of privilege or special treatment. It's when individuals take it as a matter of fact that something is owed to them. More specifically, they act and believe your neighborhood totally belongs to them and that you don't even matter. For example, over the last few years the city of Portland has encouraged people to use bicycles to commute. Many of our streets have lanes dedicated for bikes, and some streets have been set aside exclusively for bike travel. Now, don't get me wrong: I think bike riding is good for the environment and also for helping people stay fit and healthy. However, during the conversations about making Williams Avenue—where our church has been located for years—a bike street, our voices and other minority business voices were drowned out. Our comments, concerns, and critiques were ignored. In some instances, it even felt like there was a bit of hostility toward our presence. When we suggested they make a few alterations to the plan, we received emails stating we had no right to try to change things. We received unfair criticisms. We were told in so many words that we were a church, and our opinion didn't really matter. And yet our church is older and has been in the neighborhood longer than many of those who were making comments. There is nothing wrong with progress. However, when people feel so entitled that longtime stakeholders' voices in the community mean nothing, that is problematic and extremely irritating.

NAVIGATING THE MOVE

So how do we defuse our personal and corporate anger? How do we cooperate with God to receive his help with our justifiable anger?

Acknowledge that we are mad. Many times, as believers, we spiritualize away too many issues. We cloak how we feel with Bible verses, cliches, and other religious gobbledygook. Gentrification can be unjust. A moved neighborhood hurts. The insensitivity, ignorance, and entitlement of new folks in the neighborhood irk us to the core. Come on, let's admit it. Even though we love Jesus, we are mad! We are upset over what has happened. God can handle our anger. I believe he wants us to be honest about how we feel and admit it to him.

One church in Seattle had what they call a testimony service. This is where people in the congregation have the opportunity to stand and share with the rest of the congregation about how God is working in their lives. But the pastor had to remind people that they were supposed to be sharing about how God was working, because they were so mad about all that was going on in the community, they were using the testimony service to vent all their pent-up anger. The Bible does not tell us not to be angry. It tells us not to sin in our anger (Eph 4:26). So acknowledging our anger personally and corporately is a must.

Give space to let it all out. I was really struggling. I could see that the impact of gentrification was adversely affecting our congregation, but I was reluctant to dive in and truthfully address the issue. My reluctance centered around the fact that our church is racially diverse, and I didn't want to ostracize or offend the Whites in our congregation. So I wrestled with doing a sermon series on the issue. After a few months it was clear to me that I had to do it. I could see people in the church languishing because of all that had transpired. I could see their faith being challenged and their hope evaporating. So I did it. I preached a four-week series titled, Who Moved My Neighborhood? The response was overwhelming. People in the congregation were wailing over the loss, crying as if someone they loved had passed away. Others were freely acknowledging their anger in a healthy manner. When the services were over, Blacks and Whites alike were walking out of the sanctuary with tears streaming down their faces. What that sermon series did was give our church the space and the permission to authentically lament with one another. I believe it was a turning point to defuse our anger against our new community.

Pray through it. Praying about our anger and pain helps. God cares for us and will always help us. Hebrews 4:16 says, "Let us therefore come boldly to the throne of grace, that we may obtain mercy and find grace to help in time of need." When we present our need to resolve our rage, there is mercy and grace present to help us.

Keep releasing anger. Unfortunately, this is not a "one and done" situation. Even though God has greatly helped me, I still find myself struggling with anger occasionally. What I've had to do and what we all will have to do is continue to roll the anger back to God. The injustice we see is not going to vanish; the displacement that has happened is not going to be reversed. It's like when the prophet Habakkuk says, "Why do you make me look at injustice?" (Hab 1:3 NIV), and God's response to him is, in essence, "You may see injustice, but I have a plan." This may seem a bit trite, but when the anger begins to resurface, we can just say, "God, it's back again, but here it is. I'm giving my anger back to you. Thank you for having a plan and helping me today."

We cannot skip or gloss over our rage. This phase is so important for leaders to normalize in their congregations if they are going to move forward in the next phase of the process. If the rage is not dealt with, the next phase, reconciliation, will be difficult—if not impossible—to navigate.

CHAPTER 8

RECONCILIATION

The reconciliation phase of the process is where we and our church come to terms with the fact our neighborhood has moved. Although we've suffered and may be still suffering deep grief over our loss, somehow we are able to find a place of peace so that we can begin to move forward. By God's grace, we are now able to get up off the mat, stand back up on our feet, and move toward forging a new reality for our church in our new neighborhood.

Finding a place of reconciliation is a must—it is not an option! If churches remain stuck in the previous phases of the process—regular, recognition, realization, reconstruction, and rage—they will be tightly fastened in a straitjacket that binds them to their past and restricts their movement into the future, thus halting their God-given mission and muting their testimony to Jesus Christ. No healthy church in its right frame of mind—changed neighborhood or not—wants to be so anchored to the past that it fails to embrace the vibrant and life-changing mission that God has ordained for its community in this present moment.

Reconciling, or coming to terms with our moved neighborhood, is much more than a matter of a church's survival—it is about a church's ability to thrive. But reconciling is no joke, and by no stretch of the imagination is it easy. In order for a church to reconcile, it must have God's help. Pure human strength, as wonderful as it may be, and good intentions alone cannot provide the framework and the fortitude to make it happen. Divine assistance through the power of the Holy Spirit must be active for reconciliation to move from being a concept to a reality.

When it comes to reconciliation, God is a powerful helper because he himself is a reconciler. Consider for a moment the reconciliation process God put into motion to redeem the world. God created this world by his own power, but it turned its heart against him and treated him unjustly, moving outside the neighborhood of his love and perfect will into a place of death and darkness. Why did God act to reconcile this world to himself? Love. And love is what the church must have to reconcile its heart to its new neighborhood. God's love for the world led him to take certain actions for reconciliation, and these actions are also helpful for us in moving from the previous phases to a place of reconciliation.

Ephesians 2:11-18 gives us a biblical portrait of the power of reconciliation and what it looks like:

> Therefore remember that you, once Gentiles in the flesh—who are called Uncircumcision by what is called the Circumcision made in the flesh by hands—that at that time you were without Christ, being aliens from the commonwealth of Israel and strangers from the covenants of promise, having no hope and without God in the world. But now in Christ Jesus you who once were far off have been brought near by the blood of Christ. For He Himself is our peace, who has made both one, and has broken down the middle

wall of separation, having abolished in His flesh the enmity, that is, the law of commandments contained in ordinances, so as to create in Himself one new man from the two, thus making peace, and that He might reconcile them both to God in one body through the cross, thereby putting to death the enmity. And He came and preached peace to you who were afar off and to those who were near. For through Him we both have access by one Spirit to the Father.

Let me highlight a few brushstrokes of this portrait, with emphasis on the colors and textures of God's beautiful work of reconciliation. In the passage, three parties are mentioned: the Gentiles, Israel, and God. The passage emphasizes the hostility and distance that exists among them prior to Jesus' death on the cross. The Gentiles are said to be uncircumcised, foreigners, strangers from God's covenant, and without hope and God in the world. The Israelites, though heirs of the covenant of God's promises, are separated from the Gentiles and, more importantly, separated from God. Even though the Scripture says they were "near," they weren't close enough! Lastly, God is in the picture. He is the one who has been offended by both parties. However, unlike the Gentiles and the Israelites, he is working redemptively through Jesus to remove every barrier that separated the Israelite from the Gentile, and every barrier that separated the Gentile from the Israelite. And he is working to remove every wall and every hint of hostility to bring both the Gentile and the Israelite to himself. The reconciliation culminates in the making of one new person out of the two previous parties who were at odds and granting them peaceful relationship with him by his Spirit.

This picture inspires faith in God's ability to reconcile those who are at odds with one another. That's great news for our present neighborhood situation. But for God to bring reconciliation to humanity, there were certain actions he had to take: a decision, a journey, a cross, a death, and a resurrection.

RECONCILIATION REQUIRES A DECISION

God recognized there was a separation problem caused by sin, so he made a *decision* to do something about it. Our heavenly Father knew we were in big trouble and could not help ourselves, so he took it upon himself to fix the problem we caused. God could have said, "You know, I told you all not to sin, but you did it anyway, so tough!" But that's not what he did. His boundless, unlimited love for us led him to make a choice to reconcile us back to himself.

I want to point out that God did not wait until we made all our wrongs right to bring us reconciliation. He chose to help us while we were still in the doghouse, while we were still offending him with our sins, while we were dead in our transgressions. His love made him decide to reconcile us even though we had not changed. This is so important for the church to grasp: if we decide to reconcile only when the movers of our neighborhood put it back or apologize to us, chances are we will never reconcile anything. Our job as a church is to reflect the character and nature of God to the world around us, even though that world may be changing. So, in order for the reconciliation process to begin in our church, we must follow the example of our heavenly Father and choose to reconcile even while the other party is not aware of the need or willing to do anything about it. This is a choice the church must make.

It can help to develop a mantra or resolution that encapsulates God's truth and declares to our own hearts and the world what we believe is God's will and purpose for our lives. It's similar to when a couple stands in front of the pastor to get married and they respond with a hearty "I do." Those words change their lives and set their feet on a whole new path for the future. We can, of course, develop our own resolutions suitable to the ethos of our particular churches, but here's an example of one that will strengthen a church's resolve to make the decision to move in the direction of reconciliation:

We acknowledge the painful loss we have experienced in our beloved neighborhood. But we also acknowledge a loving God who chose to reconcile us to himself even when we hurt him. Therefore, we make confession and say "we do" to commit ourselves to being reconcilers in our new neighborhood. And by God's grace we will choose to follow the mission of Jesus and reflect his love to those who are around us.

Once we have nailed down our mantra, we must keep it close because we are going to need it. We will have to remind ourselves and our congregations many times of the decision we have made. But over time, something as simple as this will aid us in coming to a place of peace and resolution. It may rub some people the wrong way at first, and we may even lose a few who don't want to make the decision, but that's okay. God will work with them just like he is working with us. But we can be sure we are making the right decision to reconcile.

RECONCILIATION REQUIRES A JOURNEY

God also made a journey to reconcile us. As the Andraé Crouch song reminds us, "He left His mighty throne in glory / To bring to us redemption's story."[1] In order to redeem us, Jesus made the journey from heaven to earth. He traveled a great distance to bring us into relationship with him.

I have had the opportunity to preach in many places and in all different types of churches. One thing I've said on many occasions is, "No matter where you live, the whole earth is a ghetto compared to heaven!" I agree with the old seventies group called War when they said, "The world is a ghetto." It is a slum filled with pain, lies, racism, poverty, and broken people. It is a place that, even with all its glitz and glitter, compared to heaven is ash and sand. But Jesus was willing to make the journey and leave the beauty of a glorious heaven to come to this dark, selfish world. We are so priceless in the sight of God that he sent the most priceless one in heaven—his Son. We matter that much to him.

Your new neighborhood matters to God. Jesus made a long journey for every funny-looking person you see walking down the street. And since Jesus came so far for us, can't we go a little way to make peace with those who may just be a mile, a hundred feet, or even just a walk across the street from us? Reconciliation will require us to take steps to forge relationship and build understanding with our new neighbors. I understand it is hard and may be uncomfortable. But remember the One who journeyed for you and me and how far he had to come.

Remember the story of the women from our church who went to patronize the new ice cream shop and found a flavor called chocolate crack (see chapter seven)? Well, the story did not end with their burning anger. Once they settled down, they made their journey back across the street to the ice cream shop. This time, before they went in, they decided to bring some reconciliation as opposed to just venting their anger. Entering the store, they apologized to the owner for their reaction to the menu item. Then they were able to have an honest conversation with her. They explained why chocolate crack was inappropriate and insensitive. The owner did not have a clue about the history of the drug problem in the neighborhood, but once she understood, she gladly changed the name of that ice cream. Chocolate crack was no longer on the menu.

Another opportunity that required a journey took place with our board and two major developers. There have been too many buildings to count that have been erected in the vicinity of our church. The majority of the developers hoisted their buildings without any concern of how they might affect our church. So, it goes without saying that we didn't have a real sweet spot in our heart for developers. There were a couple of lots across from our parking lot that we desperately wanted to purchase. In fact, the owner of one of the lots came into my office while we were having a board meeting and said he would sell us the property. We were jazzed! But to make a long story short, he sold it to one of the developers instead.

When the developers began to develop two massive award-winning buildings—the 116,000-square-foot Karuna and the adjacent 36,000-square-foot Radiator building—we weren't thrilled at all. If I'm honest, we were a little bitter. So, when they came over to talk to us about our parking lot, we were of the mindset: here come these White guys trying to rip us off or something. But God was at work, and we knew we had to have a right spirit despite our strong emotions. We spent eighteen months meeting and talking with the developers, Ben and Nels. And over those months, now years, we became friends. These two men have helped Life Change Church in so many ways, I could write a whole chapter on it. First, we leased some parking spaces to them that totally worked around our rhythms. Those proceeds help keep our church afloat. For other projects we had, they gave us great advice. And on another church project, Nel's son Owen served as our contractor and donated his services. Ben has attended our services and supported other ministries in our church. The relationship we built made its way into the *New York Times*. Here's a snippet of the article that focuses on working out a deal for the parking lot and, more importantly, establishing trust.

> The developers also avoided building costly underground parking by leasing the adjacent church's surface parking lot (excluding Sundays). But it wasn't an overnight process.

"It took 18 months to negotiate that parking deal," said Ben Kaiser, who developed the Radiator project and whose architecture firm, Path Architecture, designed the building. The church was concerned, he said, about being taken advantage of. Mr. Kaiser, a volunteer member of the city's Design Commission regulating central-city building design, initially purchased the land for both the Radiator and Karuna, before selling the latter to Gabbert and Lemelson. He also lives nearby. "You can see why there's distrust," he said. "I still drive by all those acres that were torn down decades ago and are still empty." Dr. Strong of Life Change Church says he believes that while the public courtyard is nice, and the parking revenue will allow outreach to his displaced congregation, *forging trust was the most important success* [emphasis added]. "They've got this incredibly energy-efficient building, they've got the seismic-warning equipment," he said. "They get some gold stars for that."

"Many times developers will come and talk enough to get permission or a quick co-sign, and once it's done that's it," he added. "But Kaiser and Nels, they went a step further. What they've done that others have not is to try to get the pulse of the people that were there before. It wasn't always easy to develop trust, but it was their commitment to work through that process that made it happen."[2]

Journeying is the commitment to work through the process.

RECONCILIATION REQUIRES A CROSS

Without the cross of Jesus there would be no redemption. Without the cross of Jesus there would be no reconciliation. Pain and death were the required offering so we could live. Though we know this, the totality of the pain Jesus experienced carrying and dying on the cross is incomprehensible. The magnitude of carrying the cross and dying for all the sins of humanity is a burden that only God could bear. Even the glimpses the Scriptures give us of his humanity cracking under the tremendous weight don't convey to us the full trauma of his passion. However, while the pain of his suffering sent tremors through all of creation—thundering from the splinters of a wooden cross, penetrated with iron spikes, and stained with the purest blood—a cry from heaven came crystal clear, a reconciling word that reaches every listening heart, every generation, every nation, and every person, spoken in the most intimate and loving way: "I forgive you."

Reconciliation requires a cross. And a cross causes us to have to deal with pain. We don't dare compare the issues we face in a changing neighborhood to the passion of our Master. However, to a lesser degree we do experience heartbreaking pain. And we are forced to carry weight on a certain level. Many times, when we experience neighborhood injustices, our principal cry is for justice. We find ourselves in the same spirit as James and John: "Lord, they messed up our lives. Send the fire down this instant" (Lk 9:54). But following Jesus' example, we cannot allow the pain to squelch the purpose of God's heart. Even in the midst of pain, forgiveness is to be extended.

In our city I've had my hand in a lot of justice issues. I have discovered that, in people's quest for justice, forgiveness seldom enters the conversation. We are missing something in some instances. Forgiveness does not mean we abandon working on justice issues, but it does mean we can't hate the people we may be working to change. Forgiveness is not passive, either. It is not for the weak of heart. Forgiveness is hard, and that's why many people won't do it.

I once assisted Bruce Wilkinson in writing a book on forgiveness. A lady in our community got ahold of it and wanted to buy copies to give to everyone who was working in a peace coalition for our community. One of the leader's responses was that we don't need forgiveness right now. But he was absolutely wrong. Forgiveness is needed whenever a sin, offense, or transgression is present. Jesus forgave out of his place of pain; we are wise and healthy when we do likewise.

This is true even if we have been shoved around a lot. In Portland, the African American community has a lot of compounded pain because we have been shoved around so much. Here's a bit of history from 1948 until now, taken directly from the Portland Housing Bureau's report on the displacement of North and Northeast Portland.

> On Memorial Day in 1948, the Columbia rose 15 feet, turning Vanport into a lake and leaving 18,000 people homeless. One-quarter of them were African Americans, left to find their way in a city where they had never been welcome.
>
> Ten years after Vanport, the redlining policy had been removed from the real estate code, but the practice itself persisted unofficially. Seventy-three percent of Portland's black population, now in the tens of thousands, was concentrated in Albina. Limited employment opportunities for blacks meant that Albina was home to some of the city's lowest income households. As blacks were routinely denied mortgages and financing to improve their properties, the aging Albina housing stock deteriorated into dilapidation. . . .
>
> In the ensuing decades, a series of city plans would alter the face of the community that had been built there. Federal legislation in the mid-twentieth century encouraged cities to redevelop blighted areas. In Central Albina, hundreds of homes were razed to make way for the Memorial Coliseum, then Interstate 5.

In 1967, Emanuel Hospital announced plans for a new medical campus to be located in Central Albina. To make space for development, Emanuel cleared land of more than 200 properties. Strong community opposition lead to a Replacement Housing Agreement in 1971, signed by Emanuel Hospital, the Housing Authority, the Portland Development Commission, the Model Cities Citizens' Planning Board, and the City Demonstration Agency. The agreement promised 180-300 housing units would be developed as replacements for demolished homes, but those homes were never built. All told, Albina's Eliot neighborhood alone lost half of its residents—3,000 people—to involuntary displacement between 1960 and 1970. . . .

From 1990 to 2000, the number of African Americans living in the area declined by 3,800. In 2000, city planners identified 4,000 acres along North Interstate Avenue for urban renewal, establishing the city's largest urban renewal area. Although twenty urban renewal areas have existed within the city since the late 1950s, few others have included substantial residential areas. The Interstate Corridor Urban Renewal Area (ICURA), however, contains sections of 10 neighborhoods, many of them historically African American neighborhoods. In the next ten years, the population of African Americans declined by another 7,650.

Included in the report as well is a story from a person named Marion. She summarizes on a personal level all the moves the African American neighborhood has had throughout the years in Portland:

I grew up near Jefferson High School. My family tended a garden on the south side of Jefferson, across the street. Today, those lots are additional field space for the school. In the African American community, family members stay in the neighborhood to remain close to each other. As housing costs rise, families are forced to move away from each other, breaking up the community. Many families that grew up in North and Northeast Portland are now forced to move away from the neighborhoods where they have lived their entire lives. When the Vanport floods occurred, the African American community was displaced. When Emanuel Hospital was built, my community was displaced. When the Coliseum was built, my community was displaced. When the Rose Garden was built, my community was displaced. Now, with the new high-end housing and businesses getting built, my community and I are getting displaced.[3]

My goal in sharing all this information is to reiterate the point I've already been making in this book: the pain is real, and sometimes the blows are repetitive. But the blows Jesus took across his back were painful and repetitive too. And he still forgave. Now, absolutely don't just lie down and let injustices continue to happen without fighting back. Raise your voice and work hard to make a change. But above all, follow the Master's example and forgive. He has commanded us to do it, and reconciliation requires it.

RECONCILIATION REQUIRES DEATH AND RESURRECTION

Jesus' death and resurrection were part of the Father's reconciliation plan. In order for us to be reconciled to God and be restored to the relationship we were created to enjoy with God, Jesus had to die and rise from the dead. His death was the one sacrificial offering that freed us from our otherwise inescapable death sentence. The equation is simple: If Jesus doesn't die, we never live. If Jesus fails to rise from the dead, in the words of the apostle Paul, "Everything you've staked your life on is smoke and mirrors"

(1 Cor 15:14 The Message). And, I might add, reconciliation to our loving God and others never happens. But, hallelujah, Jesus did die and we do live. Jesus did rise from the dead and our lives overflow with faith, hope, and purpose, as 2 Corinthians 5:14-15 says: "For the love of Christ compels us, because we judge thus: that if One died for all, then all died; and He died for all, that those who live should live no longer for themselves, but for Him who died for them and rose again." These verses not only beautifully articulate the reality of Jesus' death and resurrection, but they also highlight the possibility of a new purpose in life for us. We no longer live life only for ourselves, but we have the glorious privilege of living for Jesus, the one who died and rose again for us!

It is important for us to understand that Jesus' death was purely voluntary on his part. By his own volition, he laid down his life for the good of all. No force on the face of the earth—military might, sickness, accident, or the cross—had the ability to snuff out the life of the Son of God. He died because he submitted to the Father's will and made the personal decision to give his life to reconcile the world. As he said, "Therefore My Father loves Me, because I lay down My life that I may take it again. No one takes it from Me, but I lay it down of Myself. I have power to lay it down, and I have power to take it again. This command I have received from My Father" (Jn 10:17-18).

Death in its purest sense is separation and loss. In Jesus' case the loss and separation were totally voluntary. Once again, I am not trying to place our experience on any level close to what Jesus experienced, but there is a principle here for reconciling our changed neighborhood. I want to be extra sensitive here because churches and their people have seen and experienced some great losses. However, to come to the place of reconciliation, there has to be a voluntary death of sorts. As difficult and painful as this is, a church has to be willing say goodbye to dreams, expectations, memories, and people. There has to be a letting go of the ideals we may be entitled to but that in reality are no longer a possibility. I'm not advocating a passive, fall-down-and-die approach but a redemptive, reconciliatory act whereby we say goodbye to life as we knew it in order to embrace the new possibilities and opportunities that await us on the other side.

In the early nineties, I attended a denominational meeting focusing on pastoral health. The speaker for the day was a popular psychologist in the area who had written a great book on holistic health. In a moment of transparency, he broke down and poured his heart out to us pastors about the painful divorce he recently experienced. He lamented the loss of his wife. It was obvious to everyone in the room that this man loved his wife. He also lamented over what the divorce cost him on a professional level. He lost speaking engagements on some of the largest platforms in the country at the time. He lost friends and many other gems that were precious to his heart. Mourning deeply, he explained to the group what he had to do to move on with his life. Sadly, he explained how he went to the exact place where he had originally proposed to his wife. As he sat there, memories flooded his mind of her joy when she accepted his proposal. He reflected on the wonderful years they spent with one another, and he lamented the death of the dreams that would never be a reality. Sitting there in the very spot where their marriage began, in his heart he held a funeral for it. He wrote a letter to his wife and to himself that essentially said, "Today I release my dreams, hopes, and expectations of our future together, and I acknowledge we are no more. So, with love and forgiveness, and anguish of heart, I release you. I release our marriage, and by the grace of God I say goodbye to the love of my heart." Talk about seeing a bunch of grown folks cry! We sure did that day, as we all entered into his loss.

His process was one of dying to what was dear to him. I've talked to dozens of community members, pastors, and politicians who have come to terms with losses in the community. Some of them have said goodbye and others are struggling to do so. Where are you in this difficult process? Where is your church? Are there places where a letter is needed to bring closure? Or are you still trying to hold on to something in your heart while God is softly saying, "Let it go"? Letting go is hard. Saying bye is difficult. But there is no resurrection without a death.

Resurrection opens us up to new possibilities for our churches and neighborhoods that cannot be seen or experienced from the other side of the grave. A power is released that shatters darkness and hopelessness. A spirit is released that empowers our churches to thrive and do the will of God in our communities. God wants our churches to experience his resurrection power in our neighborhoods. He wants lives changed and transformed by the power of the gospel of Jesus Christ. He wants the glory of his Son to permeate the painful narratives in the lives of the broken. His will is to bring us to that place. In the reconciliation process, death is not our final destination. Our final destination is resurrection.

To recap, reconciliation is the phase where we come to a place of peace within ourselves even though nothing in our external reality has changed. In our own hearts and community there is a tangible sense of God's shalom. We are comforted because we know the pathway to reconciliation. We're blessed because we can follow the roadmap of the Great Reconciler, who reconciled us to himself even when we were hostile toward him, who made a journey from heaven to earth to redeem you and me, who suffered the pain of the cross to offer forgiveness to the world, and who chose to die that there might be a resurrection to new life for all of us to experience.

Lord Jesus, I thank you for the courage of my brothers and sisters. Lord, you understand all the nuances of what a church experiences when their neighborhood moves: the heartache, the anger, the darkness. Lord, you know it all. Today I stand in prayer with them asking you to give them the strength to be reconcilers. Give them the ability to forgive, the ability to say goodbye, and the ability to make the necessary journey. But Lord, most of all give them a fresh hope. Let them know tomorrow is filled with resurrection possibilities. Give them the fortitude to hang in there and see what the end is going to be. I ask this in the name of the Great Reconciler, Jesus. Amen.

In these first chapters we've focused on what it takes for the church to find healing and to get up off the mat and back on its feet. We discussed the process that involves the phases of regular, recognition, realization, reconstruction, rage, and finally reconciliation. In the next section of the book we will explore the final phase of the process, revamp. Revamping entails addressing several strategic navigational questions. Answering these questions will empower your church to reenter and navigate your neighborhood with a fresh sense of mission and effectiveness. Figuring out how your church is going to serve your new neighborhood is challenging yet exciting.

PART 2

MAPPING YOUR FUTURE

CHAPTER 9

REVAMP

Because your neighborhood has moved, you now have the opportunity to enter into fresh new ministry opportunities and adventures. To paraphrase the old television program *Star Trek,* your church has the chance to boldly go where it hasn't gone before. Revamping is the process whereby you realign your church on multiple levels for the season of ministry that is before it.

From a scriptural perspective, this ordeal is nothing new. Throughout history, God has always called and led his servants to do new works in new places. It just happens that your church is now finding its place in his grand narrative. However, discerning exactly what that is supposed to look like and identifying the practical actions we are to take requires a bit of navigating. The good news is that the navigation doesn't have to be difficult or burdensome. God calls us to a task with what we have in hand, not with what we don't have. Therefore, with his help you already have what you need to get to work and get the job done. Discovering how your church will serve your new neighborhood is less about the solutions and more about the practices you will engage in during this season.

DISCERNMENT

Romans 12:2 describes discernment as the ability to prove what is the good and acceptable will of God. Sometimes we get hung up here because we think God is playing some type of hide-and-seek game with us. But he's not! God wants us to know and do his will more than we do. Therefore, he is eager to show us what it is we need to know.

To demystify the discernment process, there are several questions that can help guide us through the process. The first is: What do we have in our hand? Each church is uniquely gifted and graced by God (Eph 4:11-13) with strengths, talents, and abilities that God has placed at our disposal to use for his glory. One problem we face is that the trauma caused by our changed neighborhood can eclipse the rich treasures God has so richly blessed us with. Like the children of Israel, we forget God, who brought us out of Egypt with a mighty hand, who miraculously fed us and guided us though the wilderness. And, like them, the moment we stand at the brink of a new promised land (or neighborhood, in our case), we shrink back because the giants there make us look like grasshoppers. And grasshoppers we are not! We have to remember who we are, and "grasshopper" is not a part of our identity. Even if our church has suffered decline, we still have gifts. Even if a whirlwind of emotions encircles our hearts and the powers of hell resist us, we still have gifts. We only have to identify them.

My mother and father recently moved out of the house that my siblings and I grew up in. They lived there for over forty years, so moving them out was a job! One day all my siblings and I were there to help pack up the basement. Some of the stuff down there had been packed away for so long we had forgotten it existed.

Packing it up was a sweat-breaking activity, but more than that, it was a time of rediscovery. Wading through the mounds of relics, we discovered all sorts of lost treasures. We came across pictures that brought back tons of sweet memories. We discovered documents that had significance and valuable household items that were usable and irreplaceable. In fact, we found so many hidden treasures in the basement that the joy of our discoveries eclipsed the agony of moving.

Identifying the gifts and treasures God has blessed your church with will take some rummaging around in the basement, so to speak. You'll have to dig through the boxes of your history to find those gifts and talents that somehow may have gotten lost in the neighborhood move. You can either begin this process by yourself or bring a group of people together for a strategic reminiscing session. In this session you will want to *reflect* on the ministries the church has conducted in the past, *focus* on how God worked though the church in the past to touch the neighborhood, and then *analyze* what were the strengths and greatest successes of the church. You may discover, for instance, that hospitality is a gift that has been central to your church's ministry. Or you may rediscover that evangelism was once a strength. Or you may be reminded that the church has always had the grace to work with children.

I recommend making a list so everything is in writing. After you've completed your list, go through each item and ask the question: What gifts did our church need to do this particular ministry? Then follow that question with a passion inquiry like: What did we do that brought us the most joy and satisfaction? Though this is not a scientific method, it will help you rediscover the ministries you were most excited about in the past and identify the gifts God graced you with to make it happen. Rediscovering these gifts and passions, along with developing an awareness of your church's present giftings, will help to make it clear what you have in your hand. And knowing what is in your hand will shape the tangible love you can freely give to your neighborhood.

Discerning the needs of your new neighborhood is also part of the discernment process. Everyone has needs, including the new demographic around your church. Though their needs may be different from those of the previous neighborhood, needs are still present.

In our old neighborhood we had a ministry called Caring Hands. Every weekend we would fill the west side of our building with clothes and food to give to people in the neighborhood. Before the doors even opened, there would be lines of people wrapped around the corner waiting to get in. When our neighborhood changed, the lines started dwindling to the point where we stopped the ministry because no one was coming. Food and clothing were no longer a need in our community. We were now faced with the challenge of finding out what the community did need. We realized one of the gifts we have is our building, so we prayed about what we could do with it. It turned out that a woman from our church was starting a school called Kairos that would reach children in our neighborhood. So we rented them the west side of the building for the school. It was beautiful because we were helping them fulfill their mission, and their school gave us inroads in the new neighborhood.

Be courageous and find out what your neighborhood needs. Talk with people, build relationships, and get in spaces where you can listen. Feel free to experiment too. There is nothing wrong with trial and error. Try a bunch of things. If something fails, no big deal. Just step up to the plate and swing again. If a major league baseball player gets paid millions for hitting a ball three times out of ten, then what's a few whiffs?

The last point I want to highlight in the discernment process is what I call the peace variable. Colossians 3:15-17 says,

> And let the peace of God rule in your hearts, to which also you were called in one body; and be thankful. Let the word of Christ dwell in you richly in all wisdom, teaching and admonishing one another in psalms and hymns and spiritual songs, singing with grace in your hearts to the Lord. And whatever you do in word or deed, do all in the name of the Lord Jesus, giving thanks to God the Father through Him.

One of the ways God lets us know we are on point is through his peace. God's peace is the best neighborhood navigational compass that we can get our hands on. If we're going in the wrong direction, it will ding us. If we're going in the right direction in spite of the difficulties, his peace will affirm us. When Scripture says to "let the peace of God rule in your heart," it implies God's peace will serve as an inner umpire to judge our motivations, decisions, and actions, as well as help clarify the best path for us to take. This means we don't have to respond to pressures that want to force us to do too much or too little, or that make us want to go too fast or too slow, or that simply want us to go in the wrong direction.

One of my favorite Scriptures is Philippians 4:5-8. I can't tell you how many times I referenced this passage in the midst of our church's navigational journey.

> Let your gentleness be known to all men. The Lord is at hand.
>
> Be anxious for nothing, but in everything by prayer and supplication, with thanksgiving, let your requests be made known to God; and the peace of God, which surpasses all understanding, will guard your hearts and minds through Christ Jesus.
>
> Finally, brethren, whatever things are true, whatever things are noble, whatever things are just, whatever things are pure, whatever things are lovely, whatever things are of good report, if there is any virtue and if there is anything praiseworthy—meditate on these things.

We don't have to worry about a single thing—not about how we are going to reach the neighborhood, or how are we going to overcome the mountain in our way, or if we have what it takes. Prayer supersedes worry, and the fruit it produces is a trillion times better than worry. When we pray, God promises us that his peace will protect our hearts and our minds through Christ Jesus. In other words, his peace will be a garrison around our hearts and minds, shielding us from the forces that seek to derail us from pursuing his will.

I encourage you to stop and take a deep breath. Allow God's peace to fill your entire being. Your church will get the job done, and you will discern what to do. You will do so not in a crucible of stress but only under the gracious canopy of God's peace.

Finally, allowing the Holy Spirit to lead you and your church is a source of peace. Romans 8:5-6 says, "For those who live according to the flesh set their minds on the things of the flesh, but those *who live* according to the Spirit, the things of the Spirit. For to be carnally minded *is* death, but to be spiritually minded *is* life and peace."

The Spirit of God is a great guide, and he is faithful to lead us. Like the adage goes, "Where he guides, he provides," he will provide us with wisdom. He will provide us with strength. He will provide us with encouragement. He will provide us with strategy. He will provide us with comfort. And he will provide us with peace. The key to abiding in the Spirit's peace and following his lead is summed up in one word—*yield*. To yield means to joyfully surrender to his leadings and instruction, which are always grounded in Scripture. He would never lead us anywhere outside of biblical parameters. As we yield to him, what he desires will be accomplished in our churches and our neighborhoods. And his will is that our church has the ability to identify its gifts, discover what the needs are in our neighborhood, and then by his power make a connection that gloriously brings Jesus Christ to our new neighborhood.

However, yielding to the Spirit to make this connection will at times require the church to have to change to some degree. And God is faithful to make us aware of the areas in which we need to change.

CHANGE

Change is hard. Most people don't like it, and the average church doesn't want it. The congregants have worked hard to establish what is, and they've worked equally as hard to keep it that way. So, who wants change as a guest in their church? When change comes to the door of the church, there's usually no smiling greeter at the door welcoming it into the building. It is the last visitor anybody wants to see, let alone embrace. Even Jesus told us change is hard. Using the parable of a wineskin, Jesus explains that the problem lies in the preference of the palate. The old doesn't want the new because they are convinced the old is better even if they haven't tasted the new. Here are his words on the subject:

> He told them this parable: "No one tears a piece out of a new garment to patch an old one. Otherwise, they will have torn the new garment, and the patch from the new will not match the old. And no one pours new wine into old wineskins. Otherwise, the new wine will burst the skins; the wine will run out and the wineskins will be ruined. No, new wine must be poured into new wineskins. And no one after drinking old wine wants the new, for they say, 'The old is better.'" (Lk 5:36-39 NIV)

If we had a yellow marker, we could highlight two key words in Jesus' exposé—*new* and *old*. The problem of incompatibility between the new garment and the old garment, the new wineskin and the old wineskin, is the old's inflexibility to receive the new.

But the ability to change and receive the new is actually a matter of life and death. Jesus was trying to teach the hearers a new way of life sent down from heaven above. But they were anchored to what was and missed out on a life-giving moment. In their mind the old was better.

As your church considers your new neighborhood and ponders how you might have to change to reach it, know that change is more than an appeasing-your-palate ordeal. An old church in a new neighborhood unfortunately doesn't have that luxury. Understand that the future of your church depends on making the necessary changes.

Jesus' purpose in sharing that parable was not to seal the fate of "the old." His intent was for the old (nothing to do with age) to know that there was hope and that they could change and experience the new work God was doing. In ancient times, one of the ways people would extend the life of an old wineskin was to saturate it and rub it down with oil. As the skin absorbed the oil, it would expand its elasticity, making it more pliable. We have the oil of the Spirit to help our churches regain their elasticity and flexibility in order for us to effectively be a neighbor and serve our community. While these sorts of changes are difficult, there are some core truths that we hang on to that help us navigate the process of discernment and change. We now turn to each of the four core questions of the revamp phase of a moved neighborhood.

CHAPTER 10

THE VISION QUESTION

Typically, questions about vision center on the notion of *what*. What will your church look like in the future? What actions will your church take to change the future? What are your church's wildest dreams for the future? But the vision question as it relates to the church navigating in a new neighborhood is emphatically different. It is more theological in nature than visionary as it focuses on *who*—that is, God—as opposed to what.

The question the church is pressed to ask and answer correctly is: Who do you see? Or, for deeper soul searching and introspection: Are we seeing the mess we are in or are we seeing the Majesty of God? In the process of figuring out how to revamp our church and navigate in our community, seeing God is paramount. A church in a moved neighborhood without a fresh vision of God will never make it to the *what*-we-will-do stage because we must know *who* we are serving to determine what we will be doing to serve others.

Understandably, difficult times have a unique way of shrink-wrapping our view of God. The giants we face seem to grow larger in our sight while the indispensable truth that, regardless of the circumstances, we still serve a majestic God grows dim. Our ability to see God in the quagmire of changing demographics, once familiar streets that are now unrecognizable, economic challenges, housing disparities, and diminishing congregations is challenging—yet it is imperative. The ability to see God in the midst of suffering loss and enduring hardship was the secret sauce that ancient God followers used to faithfully carry out their mission to the world. Without a vision of an omnipotent God, their destinies would have crumbled. The Scriptures tell us that even Jesus and Moses needed to see the invisible One in order to fulfill their missions in the face of adverse realities (Heb 11:21; 12:2).

The call of the prophet Isaiah is a dispensary of radiant, therapeutic light that shines brightly to dispel our shaded image of the living God:

In the year that King Uzziah died, I saw the Lord sitting on a throne, high and lifted up, and the train of His robe filled the temple. Above it stood seraphim; each one had six wings: with two he covered his face, with two he covered his feet, and with two he flew. And one cried to another and said:

"Holy, holy, holy is the LORD of hosts;
The whole earth is full of His glory!"

And the posts of the door were shaken by the voice of him who cried out, and the house was filled with smoke. So I said:

"Woe is me, for I am undone!
Because I am a man of unclean lips,
And I dwell in the midst of a people of unclean lips;
For my eyes have seen the King,
The LORD of hosts."

Then one of the seraphim flew to me, having in his hand
a live coal which he had taken with the tongs from the altar.
And he touched my mouth with it, and said:

"Behold, this has touched your lips;
Your iniquity is taken away,
And your sin purged."

Also I heard the voice of the Lord, saying:

"Whom shall I send,
And who will go for Us?"

Then I said, "Here am I! Send me." (Is 6:1-8)

It's an incredible passage, but before we raise the blinds and
allow the majestic light of God to shine though to our hearts, let's
start where Isaiah begins in the text: with the death of Uzziah.

King Uzziah was not a slouch. He was one of the most suc-
cessful kings in Judah. His ascent to power came at a time when
the kingdom of Judah was defeated and languishing. In his beginnings he received the commentary reserved only for a handful of
kings mentioned in the Scriptures: "And he did *what* was right in
the sight of the LORD," (2 Chron 26:4). Because he was a God fol-
lower, God blessed him tremendously. He had astronomical military success: he was able to defeat the Philistines, Israel's
longtime nemesis. He tore down the fortress walls of their
strongest cities, Gath, Jamnia, and Ashdod. He built fortified
cities near Ashdod and in the rest of Philistia. In his campaigns
he defeated several other nations and exacted tribute from the
Ammonites. Uzziah became so powerful that his fame spread to
Egypt. During his reign he amassed an army of up to 310,000
soldiers. He equipped them with all the up-to-date technology
and weaponry. He built fortification towers in strategic places in
Jerusalem and in the country to ensure national safety. In addition
to his military prowess, he was an incredible agriculturist. Uzziah

loved farming. He developed irrigation systems and had huge herds of cattle. He encouraged people to plant vineyards in the hill country and farms on the fertile soil. Under his fifty-two-year reign, Judah enjoyed great material prosperity. So, when he died, an era had ended. And when he died, Isaiah said with his own lips, "In the year that king Uzziah died, I saw the Lord."

Who knows why it was the year of Uzziah's death that Isaiah saw the Lord. Had Isaiah's vision of God been darkened due to the glare caused by the admiration and affection of a super king? Did Isaiah idolize the king? Was his brittle soul crushed by the tumbling weight of his fallen idol? Or maybe the king's death signaled a dark storm heading Judah's way. Whatever the explanation may be, Isaiah and his fellow Judeans had suffered a great loss. And Isaiah's vision of a majestic God emerged in this difficult time—a time when Judah was in a mess.

Hopefully, knowing this brings boatloads of encouragement to your heart. Like Isaiah, our normalcy has been altered. We have not lost a king, but we have lost a neighborhood. Something inside of us and outside of us has indeed died. Our neighborhood is gone, vanished, and moved. And because of our loss we are able to sympathize with Isaiah. We understand what it is to be blinded to the majesty of God due to the mess we see in our neighborhood. But we can take heart. The death of Uzziah was not the end for Isaiah; it was his beginning, initiated with a vision of the majesty of God that spawned a new ministry that impacted Isaiah's own generation and all generations to come. Similarly, our moved neighborhood is not the end for us either. But it can be the beginning of something new God wants to do to impact the lives of others in ways beyond our imaginations.

ISAIAH'S VISION OF GOD

Isaiah's vision of God is panoramic. Helping him to grasp the whole picture of his majesty, God allows the prophet to see him from multiple angles and better understand who he is even in the midst of his personal and national crisis. To put it in my vernacular, the Lord was saying to him: "Boy, even though the world around you has moved, I want to inform you that I'm not moved. So, watch this and take a good look at me. What I will show you about who I am will rock your world!"

The vision begins with Isaiah seeing the Lord sitting on a throne. Notice the interplay here with Uzziah. Due to his death, Uzziah has vacated the throne, but despite the earthly changes, God is still on the throne. Isaiah says, "I saw the Lord." (If I were preaching in our church, I would add a taste of down-home cooking and say, "He saw the *Lawd!*") Who is the Lord? He is the one who surpasses any earthly king—past, present, or future. The Lord is the one who is unlike any other. The Lord is in a class all by himself because he is

> ➤ *Creator*—he is the maker of the heavens and earth (Gen 1–3; Prov 8:22-31),

> ➤ *Omnipotent*—he is all powerful (Gen 17:1; Job 42:2; Jer 32:17; Mt 19:26; Rev 4:8),

> ➤ *Omnipresent*—he is present everywhere (Ps 139:7-12),

> ➤ *Omniscient*—he knows it all (Ps 139:1-6),

> ➤ *Immutable*—he never changes (Mal 3:6; Jas 1:17),

> ➤ *Eternal*—he lives forever (Hab 1:2; Ps 90:4; Heb 13:8; 1 Pet 5:11),

> ➤ *Righteous/Just*—he always wants the right thing for everyone (Mt 6:33; Deut 32:4),

> ➤ *Merciful*—he gives us breaks we don't deserve (Ps 103:8; Lam 3:22-23),

> ➤ *Holy*—he is totally separate from all sin and evil (Is 6:1-5; 1 Pet 1:15-16), and

> *Love*—he cares for us on a level we can't comprehend (1 Jn 4:8, 16).

Think about this for a moment. Consider how we are awestruck when we see the mighty wonders of creation: the mountains, the oceans, the stars, the beautiful landscapes. Isaiah is not looking at the creation—he is seeing up close and personal the Creator himself. That alone puts things in a different perspective. I would imagine just seeing the Lord alone would be enough, but the vision has more. The place where Isaiah saw the Lord was also mind-boggling. He saw the Lord sitting on a throne.

A throne is the legitimized seat of sovereignty, power, and authority. The person who sits on the throne is in control of all the affairs under their jurisdiction. The throne the Lord was sitting on was not the throne of Judah or Israel. It was not the throne of the nations and the kingdoms of the world. The Lord's throne is the throne of heaven. A throne whose sphere of sovereignty and authority extends to every square inch of the universe. A throne that will never expire or be vacated because it is occupied by the King of kings and the Lord of lords. In the book of Revelation, the apostle John has a vision. He enters into the vision by invitation. God opens a door and invites John to have a glimpse into heaven. Aspects of his vision are so similar to Isaiah's that we know they were looking at the same Lord in the same place—amazing!

Revelation 4:1-3 tells us what exactly John saw:

After these things I looked, and behold, a door *standing* open in heaven. And the first voice which I heard *was* like a trumpet speaking with me, saying, "Come up here, and I will show you things which must take place after this."

Immediately I was in the Spirit; and behold, a throne set in heaven, and *One* sat on the throne. And He who sat *there was* like a jasper and a sardius stone in appearance; and there was a rainbow around the throne, in appearance like an emerald.

Like Isaiah, John too saw a throne with the Lord seated on it. However, God spoke some words in John's vision that Isaiah didn't hear: "Come up here, and I will show you what must happen after this."

Just the other day, prior to writing this chapter, someone called me and asked, "Mark, where are we in the book of Revelation?" I told them, "Your guess is as good as mine!" Just like the original readers of Revelation, those in a moved neighborhood experience a great deal of chaos and upheaval. Those reading Revelation were feeling a bit hopeless and discouraged, wondering where God was in their upended world. John's vision shows us that in a seemingly out-of-control world, Jesus still sits on the throne.

Now let's contextualize what both Isaiah and John saw for our situation. The Lord, the omnipotent, omnipresent, immutable Creator of the ends of the earth is firmly seated on the throne of the universe. He is in control. Nothing that happens on the face of the earth—no matter how monumental or miniscule—affects or changes his sovereign reign over humanity and over the affairs of our lives. He is in control and works all things for the good of those who love him.

There's much more in Isaiah's vision of God that could fill up the pages of this chapter. We could talk about the train of his robe that filled the temple, symbolizing the extent of his royalty and majesty. We could discuss what the flying creatures reveal through their reverential worship of the holy God and bold proclamation that the whole earth is filled with his glory. However, respectfully fast forwarding through the vision, we arrive at the place where Isaiah is privy to eavesdrop on the conversation of the Father, Son, and Holy Spirit. The vision has driven him to a place of repentance for his own guilt and sin, his unclean lips. And now he hears God saying, "Who will go on a mission for us? Who can we send?" By virtue of his vision of God, he is now willing and ready to go and minister to people in a neighborhood, community, and nation that is void of King Uzziah.

Seeing God preceded mission, and without a fresh vision of God, Isaiah would have had no mission. God similarly gave me a brief glimpse of himself several years ago. It has helped to fuel me and our church to serve our neighborhood and city despite all the changes we have experienced. My vision was nothing like Isaiah's, but it was still life changing.

MY VISION OF GOD

One day while driving to the church to start my workday, I was experiencing an inward disturbance. There was nothing out of the ordinary that transpired on my commute. Everything was fine. I didn't drive past Skidmore Street or have any conflict with crazy drivers or bicyclists. However, by the time I pulled into the parking lot, I was definitely feeling agitated. So as usual, I parked my car, used my key card to open the front door, and made my way to my office. It was early and I was alone in the building at the time—which was a good thing.

Once in my office, I unloaded my briefcase, pulled out my Bible, and began to pray. I distinctly remember kneeling on the sofa, clenching my fist, and screaming, "God, what's up? This ain't right—how could you have allowed our neighborhood to be hijacked like this?!" Personally, I was somewhat shocked at my own outburst because I don't usually address God in this fashion, nor did I have any intention of discussing neighborhood issues with God that morning. As I continued to pray (or should I say gripe?), more and more angst poured from my heart. A flood of emotions overwhelmed me. I reflected on the times our church prayed and tried to purchase the vacant property around us to do good work but was denied. I reminisced about the many times we prayer walked our streets, asking God to work and extend his kingdom and build his church. But now it felt like we were being squeezed out. I even started to feel animosity and disdain for the people who now daily walk through our parking lot and up and down our streets. I felt anger toward the people who utilize the new bike lanes that occupy the places on the street where our church members once parked. I was having a serious meltdown.

Obviously, I had been oblivious to volcanic activity occurring within the recesses of my soul. My prayer that morning was an eruption of sorts. What had been buried deep within was surfacing. And God was helping me to tap into what I had unknowingly been processing within myself for a long time. As Romans 8:26-27 says, "Likewise the Spirit also helps in our weaknesses. For we do not know what we should pray for as we ought, but the Spirit Himself makes intercession for us with groanings which cannot be uttered. Now He who searches the hearts knows what the mind of the Spirit *is*, because He makes intercession for the saints according to *the will* of God."

Prior to this prayer time, I'd never expressed my frustration with God or my disdainful attitude toward our new neighbors in this fashion. I had been in denial and I had most likely been masking my true emotions with some type of holy façade. You know the script: Pastors are not supposed to get fuming mad. Pastors cannot allow their emotions to get the best of them, even in personal quiet time with God. Pastors are to be a rock of Gibraltar on all occasions. Besides all that, I was too busy and preoccupied with fulfilling my pastoral duties and trying to keep the ship afloat. The chasm between my inner pain and my daily ministry was wide. I hadn't realized the severity of the blow—how bad it had hurt me or our church. So I was working through my own pain and reconciliation phases that morning.

Pastors, I want to encourage you to be vulnerable before God. That vulnerability opens you up to receive his grace to help you personally and enable you to shepherd your congregation in a transitory season. When you do, the beautiful truth expressed in the classic gospel song comes to pass: "He looked beyond my faults and saw my need."

When I took the time to stop and bring my whole self—angry and disillusioned—to God, he showed himself to me. It isn't always like this, but I often wonder if we don't see what God has been up to the entire time because we don't take time to stop and listen. While I was praying, God gave me a mental picture of a chessboard. There wasn't anything mysterious or spooky about it, nor would I deem it as a vision of biblical proportions. Simply in my mind's eye, I could visualize a regular chessboard with a game in progress. Some of the pieces were on the board and others were off. My primary observation was that the pieces on the board had been moved around. Once that observation was locked in, God immediately spoke these words to my heart: "I am sovereign, and I am in control." Sovereignty means that God possesses all power and is the ruler of all things (Ps 135:6; Dan 4:34-35). It means that God rules and works according to his eternal purpose, even through events that seem to contradict or oppose his rule.[1]

While I was kneeling there on my sofa, God gave me a gift—an answer to my prayer. He made it clear. I got the sense he was speaking these words to my heart: "Yes, Mark, I know movement has occurred in your neighborhood that deeply troubles you—movement that you cannot change or have any control over. But know, son, I am well aware of every move and everything else that is happening. I am the master mover. And what alarms you does not alarm me. I am sovereign and I am in total control of every movement occurring in your neighborhood. I have a plan and I am working. That's what's up!"

In that instant, a great sense of relief entered my heart—a relief that is still present today. And a fresh surge of hope, faith, and peace flooded my soul. It was as if God placed smelling salts under my nose to awaken me out of my blow-induced stupor. I knew there was a lot of work still to do, challenges to face. However, the burden that weighed down my heart and mind for the last couple of years was lifted. It returned to the One who is capable of bearing it—the sovereign God, who is in control even of changing neighborhoods (Mt 11:28-30). What I experienced that day was life changing. It's been a few years since that day, and that particular burden has never again overwhelmed my heart to that degree.

One thing is certain: God loves us. He loves our churches and our neighborhoods. And he knows we desperately need a vision of him. There is no simple formula here. We can read and meditate on Scriptures that declare the majesty of God. We can remind ourselves of God's faithfulness to us through our lives. But the true calling card is trusting God to open our eyes. God knows we need to see him, and he wants our church to succeed more than we do.

So, I urge you simply to ask our loving Father to open your eyes so that you may receive a fresh vision of who he is that will fuel you to move forward and navigate your church toward new possibilities in your neighborhood. Because when you have seen the Lord, the death of Uzziah (or your neighborhood) is not your ending but your springboard to a new beginning.

CHAPTER 11

THE IDENTITY QUESTION

A nsel Bourne is probably best known for providing inspiration for the Bourne Identity book and movie series. He was a nineteenth-century preacher who reported waking up one day in 1857 to find himself running a general store in Norristown, Pennsylvania. The last day he remembered was two months prior to his arrival in Norristown. It turns out he was suffering from a dissociative fugue, a cognitive disorder that can be brought on by trauma and cause a person to temporarily forget their identity. His loss of identity made him forget his calling, his family, and the neighborhood where he lived.

A moved neighborhood creates an assault on your identity. Identity is important because who you are determines what you do. It is no wonder that the battle Jesus encountered during his temptation in the wilderness with the devil was not only an attempt to make him function independently of his Father but an all-out onslaught to make him question and doubt his identity.

Matthew 4:1 tells us that after Jesus was baptized, the Spirit descended upon him like a dove, and he was driven into the wilderness to be tempted by Satan for forty days and nights. Yes, Satan tried to make him misuse his power to satisfy his own physical appetites, test God, and acquire wealth and fame. But what often goes unnoticed is the subtle assault the devil unleashed on Jesus' identity. In two of the temptations, Satan said to Jesus, "*If* you are the Son of God." Twice he used these words to inject the same poison of doubt he had successfully used on Adam and Eve and many others. His diabolical aim was to make Jesus feel conflicted about his identity and thus abort his mission.

> Then Jesus was led up by the Spirit into the wilderness to be tempted by the devil. And when He had fasted forty days and forty nights, afterward He was hungry. Now when the tempter came to Him, he said, "*If You are the Son of God*, command that these stones become bread."
>
> But He answered and said, "It is written, 'Man shall not live by bread alone, but by every word that proceeds from the mouth of God.'"
>
> Then the devil took Him up into the holy city, set Him on the pinnacle of the temple, and said to Him, "*If You are the Son of God*, throw Yourself down. For it is written:
> 'He shall give His angels charge over you,'
> and,
> 'In *their* hands they shall bear you up,
> Lest you dash your foot against a stone.'"
>
> Jesus said to him, "It is written again, 'You shall not tempt the LORD your God.'" (Mt 4:1-7, emphasis added)

As I mentioned earlier in this book, part of our personal and corporate identity is rooted in where we are from. Our geographical place of origin, or the place where our roots have gone deep, aids in shaping us. (Think Mary Magdalene, Saul of Tarsus, and even Jesus of Nazareth!) Likewise, our preexisting neighbor-hoods help to define our personal and our church's identities. I'm not talking about an unhealthy association where all our personal value and esteem are derived from where we are from and by what we do. That's a whole other topic. However, there's a healthy and natural identity-forging that comes from where we are home grown. An article on how residents cope with residential diversi-fication echoes the point:

> The physical structure of neighborhoods offers a range of features which impact upon the identities and the social re-lations of their inhabitants. In general terms, insofar as neighbourhoods constitute a meaningful location, they afford a sense of "place identity" for residents, such that their sense of belonging (or alienation) will affect how they behave within that space.

The article goes on to say,

> An influx of residents who come from different or even op-posing groups can threaten the existing neighbourhood identity. Thus, an increase in diversification could challenge the ability of neighbourhoods to support their residents by eroding supportive pre-existing social identities. For ex-ample, if incomers are perceived to have an identity that is incompatible and thus threatening to the pre-existing neighbourhood identity, existing residents might expe-rience strong feelings of existential threat or "angst" and strong antipathy towards the incoming residents.[1]

When a neighborhood is moved, it can cause an identity crisis for a church. The church can feel as if it doesn't fit within the new social construct. The church can struggle to understand the new cultural ethos, and even if some of us get it, there are still many in the congregation who don't. Where the church once had a comfortable and clear role and identity, there's now the fog of a lack of a sense of place. As an article on the impact of gentrification on neighborhoods observes:

> Social identification with a meaningful and positive social group can be key to protecting health.
>
> Social identity is not only derived from personal identity (as "I" and "me"), but can also arise as well from social identity (as "we" and "us").
>
> Groups we belong to are key aspects of who we are. There are not simply external features of our environment.
>
> We derive a range of health benefits from a sense of connection to fellow in group members and an associated sense of place in our social world.[2]

When this sense of place is lost, our adversary picks up the mic and basically blares over the PA system, "Who do you all think you are? Do you really belong here anymore?" While those may not be his exact words, somehow the church gets a message that calls its identity on the carpet, and hell does its best to sweep it away. So, when a church is in the throes of trying to navigate its course, it must ask itself the existential question: Who are we? By answering this question, the church will be empowered with a new sense of place, purpose, and confidence. Navigation requires that we hold purpose in one hand and confidence in the other. Just because our neighborhood has moved, our confidence and purpose don't have to go south. We do still have a place. We can recalibrate the assurance of identity our church had prior to things changing.

My goal in this chapter is to preach you happy. My hope is that by God's grace, the words on these pages will so fire you up that at the end of the chapter you are ready to stand up on your feet and shout, "I know who I am! I know who we are!" If I don't accomplish this, I hope at the very least that any amnesia surrounding your identity and your church's identity will vanish like the morning fog.

IMPORTANT IDENTITY MARKERS

Though many factors help shape our identity, the ultimate identity shaper for the church is God. Not our education. Not our accomplishments. Not who we know. Not our talents and giftings. Not our bank accounts. God is the identity giver, and his identity is anchored unlike anyone else's in the universe. The Scriptures tell us that he is the great I AM, the sovereign Lord over all. He told Moses, "I Am who I Am" (Ex 3:14 NIV 1984). It is because of who he is that you become who you are. Almighty God says to the children he dearly loves, "Because I am, you are." Now if God says you are, then you are! So the question is, who are you?

You are the church. Your local congregation is an integral part of God's physical and visible expression of himself on earth. You are a part of the body of Jesus Christ, connected to believers beyond the confines of your own neighborhood. You are spiritually united through the Holy Spirit to believers in heaven and on earth, which makes you members of God's family whose identity is secure. The church you are a part of, and who you are, is not an earthly, human-engineered construct. Nor is it a product of our imaginations or of our neighborhood's ingenuity. The church is God's idea and the direct object of his love and affection. The church is Jesus' beloved bride, who he will one day return for so she will be forever in his presence.

Jesus speaks powerful, defining words about the church in Matthew 16:17-18:

> Jesus answered and said to him, "Blessed are you, Simon
> Bar-Jonah, for flesh and blood has not revealed *this* to you,

but My Father who is in heaven. And I also say to you that you are Peter, and on this rock I will build My church, and the gates of Hades shall not prevail against it."

Jesus is the one building the church, and you are a part of the structure. And, more importantly, notice who he says the church belongs to. He calls it "*my* church." It belongs to him. In addition, Jesus makes the profound declaration that when he builds the church, the gates of hell will not be able to stop it.

Reflect on hell's rage that the church has had to endure throughout the centuries: the painful persecution, the difficult tribulation, the insurmountable opposition, the times when political powers have tried to annihilate it. Once I was preaching in Uganda, and after the service I was talking to a woman who was explaining the horrors the Ugandan church suffered during Idi Amin's reign of terror. She remembered being in a church service as a little girl when out of nowhere soldiers broke down the door and began firing machine guns at everyone in the building. In that situation, the good news was that God miraculously protected everyone. But there have been countless cases where followers of Jesus have paid the price with their lives and exited this temporal life to receive their eternal reward. The stories of what the church has had to endure are countless. Think even about the disciples when Jesus died. They had followed this man for over three years, and he made all these promises, and then he died on a cross. How would they still manage to believe after such a traumatic event occurred? I'll tell you how: the words of Jesus are true. He said he would build his church and the gates of hell *would not* prevail against it. Despite hell's best blows, it has not—nor will it ever be able to—overcome the church.

You are the church, and the gates of hell will not prevail against you. The blow suffered from a moved neighborhood does not have the force to knock you down for the count. You don't have a glass jaw. Your jaw is made of the substance of stone that the builders rejected that has now become the chief cornerstone—the Lord Jesus himself. So rid yourself of any inferiority complexes that have invaded your identity consciousness and boldly affirm the truth about whose you are—the truth about what you are. You belong to God and you are the church.

You are the salt of the earth and the light of the world. Jesus tells us:

> You are the salt of the earth; but if the salt loses its flavor, how shall it be seasoned? It is then good for nothing but to be thrown out and trampled underfoot by men.
>
> You are the light of the world. A city that is set on a hill cannot be hidden. Nor do they light a lamp and put it under a basket, but on a lampstand, and it gives light to all *who are* in the house. Let your light so shine before men, that they may see your good works and glorify your Father in heaven.

In other words, we are needed! Who we are and what we provide is needed in our neighborhood. I can speak firsthand about the debilitating feeling of irrelevance a person can experience when they are in the throes of neighborhood transition. If I were to dump all my previous boxes of inferiority and garbage bags of insignificance on the floor, they would take up half my space. However, we must come to terms with the reality that even if our neighborhood changes, who we are at our core does not. We were the salt of the earth when our neighborhood was normal. We are still the salt of the earth even though it has changed. We were the light of the world, a city on a hill, when our neighborhood was normal. We are still the light of the world and a city on a hill that cannot be hidden even though things have changed. According to Jesus, the world around us is still in desperate need of salt and light. And our churches provide those necessary elements because that is who we are.

You are built for such a time as this. One of my favorite inspirational stories in Scripture is that of Esther. The story centers around an orphaned girl who was raised by her cousin Mordecai. She and Mordecai were living in a foreign country, and by the providence of Almighty God, Esther became the queen of Persia. In an unfortunate string of events, it was brought to Esther's attention that Haman, a high-ranking official, had devised a plan to destroy Esther's people, the Jews. Esther then faced a serious predicament. She was the only one who could thwart Haman's plan, but to do so could cost her life. To help her do the right thing, Mordecai encouraged her by saying (and I paraphrase), "Girl, you were built for this. You have entered the kingdom at this moment for this exact purpose." Esther then went before the king, interceded for her people, and saved their lives.

Like Esther, your church was built for this moment of crisis in your neighborhood. You are not where you are by accident. Perhaps you have come into your neighborhood for such a time as this. Even more so, you are built for this. Listen to the affirming words in Ephesians 2:8-10 (NIV): "For it is by grace you have been saved, through faith—and this not from yourselves, it is the gift of God—not by works, so that no one can boast. For we are God's handiwork, created in Christ Jesus to do good works, which God prepared in advance for us to do." In other words, God's saving activity in your life is purposeful. He saved you by his grace. And, miraculously, in that saving process he fashioned you to be an instrument to do good works through Jesus—works that he prepared for you to do before the foundation of the world. This means that prior to your neighborhood moving, God had already anticipated all the changes and fashioned and equipped you with all the gifts and graces you need to do good works even in your new environment. You were built for this a long time ago! Recognizing this is a great identity booster.

You are a special people. Labeling is inherent with gentrification. We have names for the gentrifiers, and we place labels on those who live in neighborhoods that have been gentrified. Many of the labels placed on those residents of gentrified neighborhoods carry with them a negative connotation. They are deemed poor, powerless, and pitied people. When you live constantly under such a shadow, it becomes difficult to keep the dark clouds from shrouding your true identity. God doesn't call you poor or powerless people, nor in his eyes are you people to be pitied. Yes, we are people in need of mercy like everyone else. But nix the pity. The way God describes the church breaks through the clouds like the bright noonday sun: "But you are a chosen people, a royal priesthood, a holy nation, God's special possession, that you may declare the praises of him who called you out of darkness into his wonderful light. Once you were not a people, but now you are the people of God; once you had not received mercy, but now you have received mercy" (1 Pet 2:9-10 NIV).

God says you are

> A chosen people—a people he has handpicked for himself,

> A royal priesthood—a people he has chosen to serve him and do his will,

> A holy nation—a people exclusively apart for God alone,

> A chosen generation—a people belonging to God, and

> A community of worshipers—a people who declares the praises of God.

Truthfully, the way your neighborhood is now, it will not remain forever. A time will come when someone will be waving goodbye to it as well. But that has absolutely no bearing on your God-given identity. You will always be a chosen people, a royal priesthood, a holy nation, a chosen generation, a community that brings praise to God.

You are a people deeply loved by God. God's deep love for us is the glue that holds all the pieces of our fractured identities together. His love is the anchor of our identity. We are the church because he loves us. We are salt and light because he loves us. We are built for such a time as this because he loves us. And we are a special people because he loves us. God's incredible love for us is like an oversized comforter that wraps all around us and gives us the security to know that whatever befalls us, we are loved by him.

Justin Taylor tells the story of George Matheson, who penned the famous hymn, "O Love That Will Not Let Me Go." Matheson had suffered many losses, but through it all, he was secure in the fact that God's love would never let him go. Taylor writes:

> At age 20 George Matheson (1842-1906) was engaged to be married but began going blind. When he broke the news to his fiancée, she decided she could not go through life with a blind husband. She left him. Before losing his sight, he had written two books of theology and some feel that if he had retained his sight he could have been the greatest leader of the church of Scotland in his day.

A special providence was that George's sister offered to care for him. With her help, George left the world of academia for pastoral ministry and wound up preaching to fifteen hundred people each week. The day came, however, in 1882, when his sister fell in love and prepared for marriage herself. The evening before the wedding, George's whole family had left to get ready for the next day's celebration. He was alone and facing the prospect of living the rest of his life without the one person who had come through for him. On top of this, he was doubtless reflecting on his own aborted wedding twenty years earlier. It is not hard to imagine the fresh waves of grief washing over him that night.

In the darkness of that moment, George Matheson wrote this hymn. He remarked afterward that it took him five minutes and that it was the only hymn he ever wrote that required no editing.[3]

> O Love that will not let me go,
> I rest my weary soul in thee;
> I give thee back the life I owe,
> That in thine ocean depths its flow
> May richer, fuller be.
>
> O Light that foll'west all my way,
> I yield my flick'ring torch to thee;
> My heart restores its borrowed ray,
> That in thy sunshine's blaze its day,
> May brighter, fairer be.[4]

In spite of all his pain and struggle, he was sure about God's unyielding love for him. This intimate knowledge made his adversities powerless to strip him from his foundational identity anchor, which was "I am loved by God." Knowing we are loved by God is our identity anchor too. When understand how much he loves us, nothing will be able to change our minds.

Paul helps us understand the power of this truth:

> Who shall separate us from the love of Christ? Shall tribulation, or distress, or persecution, or famine, or nakedness, or peril, or sword? As it is written:
>
>> "For Your sake we are killed all day long;
>> We are accounted as sheep for the slaughter."
>
> Yet in all these things we are more than conquerors through Him who loved us. For I am persuaded that neither death nor life, nor angels nor principalities nor powers, nor things present nor things to come, nor height nor depth, nor any other created thing, shall be able to separate us from the love of God which is in Christ Jesus our Lord. (Rom 8:35-39)

Although a moved neighborhood is not on the list, you get the message. You are deeply loved by God always. So without reservation you can say boldly in your heart, "I am loved by God. Yes, that is who I am, and who we are!"

IMPLEMENTING A BIBLICAL IDENTITY

During the Who Moved My Neighborhood? series I preached at our church, the Spirit of God showed up in a beautiful way. God knew the identity struggle we were experiencing, and in his love, he met us. That morning the topic was, "Who Am I?" We covered the forces that were at work to shape our identity and discussed how we needed to be aware of each of these forces and what they could produce in our lives and in our church. At the end of the message I decided to do something I typically don't do. I had prepared seven "I am" statements, and I asked the congregation to make these statements of declaration with me. Honestly, I didn't know what to expect. At first people were looking at me like, "What in the world is pastor doing this morning?" But we made the first declaration, then the second and third. By the time we made it to the last ones, the church erupted. All our voices together sounded like a mighty army. I looked out into the congregation and saw that people had their hands in the air with tears streaming down their faces, declaring with boldness who God said they were. In that moment a tangible shift took place in our church: false identities were broken and hope and light came through. A heaviness was lifted off the body. What happened after that was purely organic. I had no plan for those declarations after that Sunday, but God did. People in the congregation began to take them and share them with their friends. Our prayer team began to use them in our daily morning prayer meetings. You could also hear other people using the "I am" terminology in their congregations.

I encourage you to seek God's direction for ways to integrate the identity truths we've talked about in this chapter into your church's life. Discern what is the best vehicle for you to use and go for it. Frequently remind your church of their identity and share this information though different mediums (e.g., Bible study, preaching, handouts, apps). Follow the leading of the Holy Spirit and come up with ideas that will resonate with your church community.

Now that we have answered the vision question and the identity questions, it is time to address the purpose question: What is our mission?

CHAPTER 12

THE PURPOSE QUESTION

Knowing why your local church exists is a must. Failing to understand your God-given purpose is not a luxury you are afforded, especially if your church is trying to navigate its way through the terrain of a changed neighborhood. But during these transitions a church's mission can get lost, buried beneath the mounds of dirt heaped on it from all the neighborhood excavation and shifting. If this has happened to you and your church, you will need to get out the shovel and do the hard work of digging until you find it again. Mission provides your church with purpose muscle. Mission furnishes the very reason for your existence. Mission thrusts you out of the starting blocks. Mission keeps you going by fueling your every stride and action. Mission allows you to see the tape at the finish line by helping to set the goal you are striving for. Mission tells you why your neighborhood and the world need your church.

The importance of mission awareness is seen in Jesus' life and ministry. One of the first sermons Jesus preached was in his hometown of Nazareth. Actually, it was not so much a sermon as a public reading that focused on his mission. He read a passage from Isaiah 61:

> The Spirit of the LORD is upon Me,
> Because He has anointed Me
> To preach the gospel to the poor;
> He has sent Me to heal the brokenhearted,
> To proclaim liberty to the captives
> And recovery of sight to the blind,
> To set at liberty those who are oppressed;
> To proclaim the acceptable year of the LORD. (Lk 4:18-19)

If we study Jesus' earthly ministry, we see that he lived out and fulfilled his mission. From start to finish, he never allowed his mission to be buried or obscured from his sight. And even though Jesus's ministry did not turn out the way anyone expected, through all he experienced—persecutions, accusations, misunderstanding, abandonment, disappointment, and even death—he was always missionally on point. He continued to preach the gospel to the poor, heal the brokenhearted, proclaim liberty to the captives, give sight to the blind, give freedom to the oppressed, and proclaim the acceptable year of the Lord. Although we are not Jesus, by his grace we can do our best to follow his example. So let's get our shovels out and start to dig.

EMERALD CITY BIBLE FELLOWSHIP

In 1984, Pastor Harvey Drake and his wife, Andrea, moved from the San Francisco Bay area to Seattle, Washington. Three years later, in 1987, they founded the Emerald City Outreach and Emerald City Bible Fellowship (ECBF). A critical component fueling Pastor Harvey's desire to plant the church was his passion to address the issues that were plaguing the African American families. To accomplish this objective, he made sure the value of helping this particular demographic was woven into the fabric of the church's mission. Though helping the African American community was the driving force of the church's mission, the composition of the church is mixed. The membership of ECBF is 40 percent African American and 40 percent White, with the remaining 20 percent consisting of Samoan, Chinese, Ethiopian, East Indian, and Spanish people. Amazingly, this diverse congregation was totally on board with the mission and clear as to the direction they were going—until something happened.

In their neighborhood, two of the largest public housing projects were converted into mixed-usage, income-producing properties, which means that many lower income families and individuals were pushed out. Pastor Harvey said that the available units for housing went down from twelve hundred to three hundred. House prices began to soar as well. Homes that went for $460,000 were now selling like hotcakes for over $700,000. The youth pastor of the church was basically renting a room for $1200 per month. For longtime homeowners, this was problematic because all the development was driving up the taxes on their properties, making it difficult for them to stay in their homes. Many simply had no choice but to sell their homes and move—often as far away as seven to twenty miles south—to find affordable housing.

Like a domino effect, the shifting neighborhood began to affect the racial composition of the schools in the area. Prior to the neighborhood moving, many of the school's kids were bused in. Now that things have changed, they have decided to stop busing, so schools that were once caramel in color are now white. Not only have schools changed but so has Columbia City. At one time, Columbia City was a mecca for Black folks in Washington, but that is no longer the case. According to Pastor Harvey, Columbia City has become totally gentrified. It's loaded with new businesses, a new theater, and new restaurants that are very expensive. The neighborhood has changed so much that the fitness center they built to serve lower income families is now mostly being used by the new residents in the neighborhood.

The moving of the neighborhood sent tremors through ECBF. Their identity was shaken, and their mission was buried underneath the mounds of displaced neighborhood debris. The good news in all of this is that the church's leadership was wise enough to know they had to reexamine their mission if they were going to successfully navigate the church into the future. So Pastor Harvey and the leadership team took out their shovels and started digging.

Pastor Harvey shared with me several ways their church went about reviving their mission. His insights are helpful for all of us who are in the midst of neighborhood transition.

Intentionality. The first piece of wisdom he offers is the need for *intentionality*. If the church is going to recover its sense of mission, it has to be intentional about it. Intentionality prioritizes and creates a sense of urgency to address mission issues. It sets the expectation and locks in the mindset that the church is going to expend the energy to do the work. Without intentionality, the church risks simply spinning its wheels in the mud and going nowhere. Mud-spinning is an easy trap to fall into for a couple of reasons. First, there are so many dynamics and issues a church faces when it is gentrified, it is easy to overlook the priority of mission. Helping congregants adapt to the newness now affecting their daily lives is a challenge. Juggling church finances, dealing with a declining membership, and other pressing issues take up a lot of our ministry bandwidth.

Second, sometimes a church doesn't even know where to begin to fix the problem, and in the grand scheme of things, analyzing its mission may not seem too important. But it is very important.

In fact, it is one thing the church does have control over. The church may not have authority over the development in the neighborhood nor over the other gentrifying forces. But the church does have control over its mission. The church through the guidance of the Spirit must dictate what its mission will be, rather than allowing outside pressures or influences to do so. The only way for the church to prevent this is to be intentional about making its mission front and center.

Conversation. Along with intentionality is the need for robust conversation. Changing the inflection of his voice, Pastor Harvey said to me, "We've had some serious conversations about who's our target audience." When the church began, such a conversation wasn't necessary. The church was located in the heart of the Black neighborhood and the mission was apropos for the church setting—it was a no-brainer. Now, however, the church is in a White neighborhood, so the question must be raised, though you can image the tensions present in this conversation: the new versus the old, what God said to us in the past and what he is saying to us now, the belief that the new people need Jesus just as much as anyone, and on and on. Pastor Harvey commented that people have to develop tough skin because some of these conversations are hard to have. But nevertheless, they must happen.

I have learned from my pastoral experience that sometimes when a leadership team has to work through issues, there's a temptation to take disagreements or hard questions personally, as if the inquiry is addressed to you personally and not the issue. If we can keep in mind that the issue is not personal—and that we are a team working together to discover the mind of God on a hard issue—we can arrive at a solution that is in line with the good and acceptable will of God. So, like ECBF, let's find the courage and the thick skin to have these missiological conversations about our church's future.

Reeducation. Since the church most likely has new members who were not present at the conception of the church, as well as younger ones who may not be aware of all that has transpired, *reeducation* must take place. The revitalizing of mission is more than a boardroom endeavor. The entire church has to be able to touch, see, and taste the mission. One of the ways Pastor Harvey has done this is through casual conversations. He enjoys having personal conversations with the millennials in his church. Through these conversations, he is able to explain that the neighborhood was not always like this. He is able to walk them down a road where they can see all the landmarks and nuances that formed the cradle that their church was born in. Expanding their frame of reference empowers them to grasp the church's mission as well as deepen their roots and buy in to what used to be and what is now. Resisting the assumption that the congregation knows it all or that the leadership knows it all is a good move. Knowing that everyone involved has room to learn gives the church the opportunity to evolve missionally and grow together.

So, decide what is important for your church to know about its mission. There may be historical information to share—perhaps some of those defining "Ebenezer" moments when God worked in the church in a powerful way. There may be scriptural truths that need to be communicated. Reeducation is needed not only in the church but also in the community outside its four walls.

Engagement. Pastor Harvey was also emphatic about the need for the church to *engage* with the new neighborhood. Even though ECBF has maintained its mission component to help African American families, they understand they also have a biblical mandate to share Christ with their new neighbors. For the church to engage the community, it has to go outside its four walls and be in the places where the new neighbors are. Of course, this can be intimidating. And it is a hard ask of certain long-term members of the church because you are asking them to love the ones they hold responsible for moving everyone else out of the hood. But who said mission was easy and doesn't cost us anything?

Prayer. Finally, Pastor Harvey stressed the importance of *prayer*. I loved what he said about it: "Through prayer we were able to stop boxing with God and start rolling with God." What a great statement! Prayer brings us to a place of surrender and submission so we can accept God's will and do it. We could all use a little less fight and a little more surrender. That is the posture that makes God's mission for a church not only a possibility but a reality. And according to Pastor Harvey, prayer bends our heart into the right position.

One other big issue a church faces when it grapples with its mission in a moved neighborhood is whether the church should stay there or move out with the rest of the neighborhood. This is a huge missional question. Pastor Harvey indicated to me this question was on the table for his church too. As Alvin Sanders, the president and CEO of World Impact, said, "Every single church is called to make disciples. . . . *It has to decide: is it there to reach its community even if its community changes? That's really the biggest pressure.*"[1]

It is a big pressure! No church in its right mind would disagree that it is there to reach its neighborhood. But when its neighborhood is gone, what is it supposed to do? This is a question our church has discussed for the last couple of years. It isn't easy, and personally I believe there isn't just one right or wrong answer. However, there can be wrong motives for either staying or leaving. There are often conflicting expectations from neighborhood residents, old and new, about what the church should do. Some of the people who have the strongest opinions have never attended a worship service at the church, but they act as if they are the prophet Elijah bringing you a direct word from the Lord. Actually, most opinions that come our way have nothing to do with the work of Jesus Christ but are all about maintaining a Black presence in the community. I might be on thin ice here, but while I totally believe in the importance of keeping and maintaining a Black presence in North Portland, that is not the sole reason our church or any other church should stay in a neighborhood. The church is to be a redemption center, and it cannot be a redemption center if neighborhood color preservation is on the throne instead of Jesus. I make this statement cautiously because people could think that I'm just a sellout, but I say it anyway because it is the gospel truth.

On the other hand, there are people who will tell you to get the church out of there because there are too many White people, or too many Spanish, or Black, or so on. If God is speaking to your church and telling you that your ethnic presence is needed, then don't move! Your church has to discern his will, and like Mary the mother of Jesus told the servants at the wedding in Cana, "Whatever he tells you to do, do it!" You cannot allow issues purely of race determine what your church's next steps should be. It may factor into your mission, but if so, take a hard look at what you are going to do, and then make sure it is what Jesus wants you to do.

Along the lines of moving, some churches have merged with other churches. This has worked great in some cases and has been more difficult in others. Other churches have started satellite churches in areas where old neighborhood residents have moved to. So there are some other options available besides simply staying or moving.

Another motivation to move is money. Most churches in gentrified areas own prime property, and developers are salivating to lap it up. In some instances, multiple millions of dollars are on the table. But do you move the church for a boatload of money? Is that the right motivation? Pastor Tipton of the First Baptist

Church in East Nashville has received repeated offers to sell the church for lots of money, but he says, "I don't think God did all of that for us then to say, 'Well, let's just go on and take the highest bid, and we'll go find something else.' . . . I just don't think that's what God has for us."

Then there is the other side of the coin: Do you hold on to the property and not sell because you refuse to let developers buy you out like they have bought out everyone else? Do you stand your ground whatever the cost? What if giving up the ground is God's best for the mission of the church? Or do you cling to the building because of deep emotional attachment? Maybe all the precious memories are tying you down and keeping you from moving.

These are life-altering choices that will have a powerful effect on your congregation and your neighborhood. Once you make them, they will be impossible to undo. As a fellow neighborhood navigator, I know what you are going through. I've been there and, in some fashion, I am still there now as our leadership is still in this process. I believe that the decision of staying or moving from your neighborhood is one of the hardest you will have to make. And staying on track missionally is difficult because yielding to the wrong motivations has the potential to place the church on the wrong missional path. But as we discussed in the chapter on identity, you were built for such a time as this.

So whether your church goes or stays, some deep soul-searching is required. Your leadership will have to carefully examine its motivations. Seeking wise counsel is also important. Talk to people who have a voice in the life of your church. Have conversations with the wise, seasoned people in your congregation, and talk to leaders of other churches that have stayed and leaders of churches that have gone. Their wisdom could prove to be extremely beneficial to you and your community. Scripture tells us that in the multitude of counsel there is safety. So be safe. Most of all, don't rush. Allow the peace of God to guide and comfort your heart through the process. And once you make your decision, go for it. Don't second-guess your decision. Forget the what ifs. You made your decision in the godliest way possible, so trust God and know that whether you decide to stay in your neighborhood or move out, Jesus is with you! You and your congregation have the absolute freedom in Jesus to navigate the church any way the Master leads. So be free to choose and fulfill your mission.

CHAPTER 13

THE RELATIONAL QUESTION

The second greatest commandment in Scripture is to love your neighbor as you love yourself (Mt 22:39). This command is only preceded by the one to love God with the totality of your being. The first command generally raises no objections. What believer would argue against the primacy of loving God? But the second command is a bit trickier. Suppose you don't even like your neighbor—how in the world are you going to love them? If your neighbor is a complete jerk, are you still supposed to have a soft spot in your heart for them? What about if your new neighbor helped to force out of the neighborhood your old neighbor, who you did love? Does the second commandment still apply to them? Or suppose you don't even know who your neighbors are. What do you do then?

This bring us to the relational question: Who is my neighbor? This question hurls relational passivity and indifference out the window and pushes the church to develop meaningful relational engagement and service. So to navigate our church effectively in a moved neighborhood, we would be wise to pose this same question that a man tossed at Jesus over two thousand years ago.

128 of MAPPING YOUR FUTURE

The aim of this chapter is not to give you demographic descriptions of the people who have moved next door to your church. There are many great resources out there that can help with that. My goal is to share with you some relational axioms that will help move your church into the neighborhood spaces where you are in close enough proximity to find out for yourself who your neighbors are. The answer Jesus gave to the ancient inquirer lays the relational groundwork for us today and poses another question that may have eluded our thinking.

Here's the account from Luke 10:29-37:

> But he, wanting to justify himself, said to Jesus, "And who is my neighbor?"
>
> Then Jesus answered and said: "A certain man went down from Jerusalem to Jericho, and fell among thieves, who stripped him of his clothing, wounded him, and departed, leaving him half dead. Now by chance a certain priest came down that road. And when he saw him, he passed by on the other side. Likewise a Levite, when he arrived at the place, came and looked, and passed by on the other side. But a certain Samaritan, as he journeyed, came where he was. And when he saw him, he had compassion. So he went to him and bandaged his wounds, pouring on oil and wine; and he set him on his own animal, brought him to an inn, and took care of him. On the next day, when he departed, he took out two denarii, gave them to the innkeeper, and said to him, 'Take care of him; and whatever more you spend, when I come again, I will repay you.' So which of these three do you think was neighbor to him who fell among the thieves?"
>
> And he said, "He who showed mercy on him."
>
> Then Jesus said to him, "Go and do likewise."

The most significant conclusion we can draw from Jesus' answer is that being neighborly is a *choice*. Everyone makes a choice in this story—not just the priest and the Levite but the Samaritan too. Samaritans were an ethnic group that were looked on with disdain in biblical times. They were regarded as dogs, half-breeds, and illegitimate. But the Samaritan, a human being, had to make a choice to be neighborly or not. And the same goes for us today.

We have to make a choice as a church to be neighborly or not to those around us. And this should not be a difficult choice—it is a no-brainer. We know what Jesus wants us to do. And we are all well aware of the second commandment: love your neighbor as yourself. Yet there is a risk that our churches could end up on the wrong side of the road, so to speak, where we go straight to our religious responsibilities but miss the very heart and command of God on the way.

There are three axioms we can learn from this passage. If we follow them, we won't strike out like the priest and the Levite but will smash the ball out of the neighborhood ballpark like the Samaritan.

THREE AXIOMS

The first axiom is *seeing is being*. When we see a person as a neighbor, we will be present. In the story, each individual saw the poor man on the Jericho Road. But did the priest and the Levite *really* see him? They saw someone sprawled out on the street in dire straits, but they did not recognize him as a person who God loves or as a neighbor in need. That's why they were not present and kept on their merry religious way. The Samaritan, however, genuinely saw the man, which compelled him to cross the street and be present.

When a church truly sees its neighbors, it will be physically present for them. We can't be good neighbors if we are not present, and we can't be present if we fail to see our neighbors. We need to see them and figure out how to cross the road to be with them. Sometimes we make this harder than it needs to be.

First Baptist Church in Georgetown is a 150-year-old church that is now in a completely gentrified neighborhood. But they get it. They see their neighbors and make the effort to be present. Their pastor says, "Adapting to gentrification isn't as much about the neighborhood as it is about the church's commitment to serve."[1] In order to serve, you have to see and be present. One thing the church does is a cookout for the community. This gives the neighbors an opportunity to be with the church and the church a chance to be with the neighbors. They also leave the church doors open when they are having a concert or some other event that may be of interest to the community. One week they had twelve neighbors walk through the door.

One thing I did in our church—though it was extremely uncomfortable for me—was walk around and introduce myself and the church to the new neighbors. Doing this sort of thing is not my cup of tea—or coffee for that matter! But I was burdened. There was a time I knew almost every person who lived on the block, but now that's not the case. Some of the conversations I had were great. I at least got to know their names and let them know that, if there was any way the church could serve them, it would be our pleasure to do so. So to be a neighbor requires us to see and be.

The second axiom is *caring is sharing*. Because he cared, the Samaritan man shared with his neighbor: "So he went to him and bandaged his wounds, pouring on oil and wine; and he set him on his own animal, brought him to an inn, and took care of him. On the next day, when he departed, he took out two denarii, gave them to the innkeeper, and said to him, 'Take care of him; and whatever more you spend, when I come again, I will repay you'" (Lk 10:34-35).

Look at the actions flowing from his neighborly compassion. He bandages the man's wounds. He uses his own resources—his oil and his wine that cost him money. He placed the man on his own animal while he walked. He took the man to a place where he could recoup, and he paid the bill. Also, he was willing to follow up on the man's condition with the innkeeper. He shared his time, his resources, his money, and his reputation—all because he cared for his neighbor.

Church, do we care about the neighbors around us? Does the compassion of Jesus fill our hearts for them so we are moved to share what Jesus has given us with them? What are we willing to share and what do we need to share—our time, our resources, our money? If we are truly neighbors, something of substance should be flowing from our hearts.

Axiom three is *knowing is going*. Jesus concludes his discourse on being a neighbor with the words, "Go and do likewise" (Mt 10:37). Jesus had asked the lawyer who he thought was the real neighbor to the man who fell among the thieves. The lawyer replied that it was the man who had mercy on him. Once the man answered correctly, Jesus told him to go and do likewise. In other words, "You go now and be a good neighbor!" Here is where a pivotal navigational twist occurs. It provides the biblical shove the church needs to move from the pew into the places where the people in the neighborhood are.

Remember that the conversation started with the lawyer asking Jesus, "Who is my neighbor?" That question placed the focus not on the lawyer but on the people around him. The question relieved him of any neighbor responsibilities. He was basically asking, "Are my neighbors Jews, Samaritans, Black people, White people, Hispanic people, Asian people?" But the way Jesus answered the question placed the neighbor responsibility squarely back on him. The Samaritan man who exemplifies excellent neighbor characteristics doesn't just shine a light on who is the neighbor is, but he also exemplifies what a neighbor does. In essence Jesus changes the question—*who* is my neighbor?—to a command—*you go be a neighbor!*

This is a paradigm shift for those of us who are serving in gentrified neighborhoods. Let's be honest: we spend a lot of time talking about "them" and "they." Jesus is letting us know it is not about "them" and "they." It's about us being the neighbor he has called us to be. It is about us fulfilling the second command to love our neighbor as we love ourselves. And finally, it's about us going and doing likewise. It's about us being the neighbors who shine the light of Jesus in the dark world around us. When we know, we will go.

FOUR WILLS

When navigating change, there are four "wills" that will empower the church to roll into the neighborhood. These wills are based on what it took for Peter, a Jew, to go on a journey to Cornelius the Gentile's home (Acts 10). By going, Peter entered a new "neighborhood," so to speak, that he had never entered before. These wills helped Peter, and they can help you too.

First is the will to *journey into the neighborhood* (Acts 10:19-20). Willingness is the equivalent of shifting your car gear from park to drive. Before Peter went to Cornelius's home, he was parked in his culture, his religion, and his upbringing. But once the Spirit moved, the gear shifted and he was willing to go even to a place that was out of bounds for him and his culture. He went knowing that his actions would be grossly misunderstood by his own community. But God was there with him and the neighbor he went to see.

Second is the will *to be guided* (Acts 10:19-26). Cornelius sent men to bring Peter to his home, and Peter had to be willing to allow these men to lead him. As we endeavor to be neighbors, there are times when we are going to have to let someone guide us to the place that we need to be in order to be good neighbors.

The guides may be foreign to us, but they know something about the new terrain of our neighborhood that we don't. Being teachable and leadable is essential.

Next is the will *to learn from our neighbors* (Acts 10:27-33). As we engage with the people in our neighborhood, we can't have the mindset that we are the sole teacher. While there are truths we can teach, there is much we can learn from them too. When Peter went to Cornelius's house, he went to teach, but he was startled by what he learned.

Finally, there is the will *to give what we have* (Acts 10:34-43). Jesus has given us tremendous blessings, and we are to share those with our neighbors. Peter shared what he had received from the Lord with Cornelius. And Cornelius and his whole house gladly received what he had to offer. Sure, there will be people who won't receive what we are offering, but there will also be some like Cornelius who will![2]

Your neighborhood needs your church. And your church has the potential to be the best neighbor that the people in your neighborhood will ever have. What an opportunity! So what are you waiting for? You have a new set of wheels, so get going; someone is waiting for a good neighbor to show up. They are waiting for what you have to share with them.

As you go, you may discover that you are not the only one showing up. God will show up too—and you may be surprised by what he does!

CHAPTER 14

NAVIGATIONAL SURPRISES

This is the gospel truth: God still loves the world. His heart still yearns at this present moment to bring a distant humanity into an intimate relationship with him. The same incredible love that compelled him to send his beloved Son to a hostile world to die on the cross for our sins is active today, working to give life to the lifeless, hope to the hopeless, and love to the unloved. Within the embrace of God's incredible and unexplainable love for the world is your neighborhood. It is the apple of his eye, the community of his divine affection. There are times when his love is so great it will bust through boundaries of our plans, ideas, and abilities, and do something through us that will leave us awestruck. These divine navigational surprises happen because Almighty God wants to reach down and give your neighbor a redeeming kiss to say how much he loves you. Our church received one of these surprises, and we are still rejoicing in awe and amazement a few years later.

When our neighborhood moved, the majority of the residents moved east to Gresham, Oregon. Gresham was nicknamed "the Numbers" by residents of North Portland because the street numbers in the east go from 140th to 200th (as opposed to North Portland where most live between 6th and 15th Street). Before our neighborhood moved, Gresham was a pretty "vanilla" city, but due to the mass exodus from North Portland, that is no longer the case. We struggled as a church with what we should do. Should we sell our building and move to Gresham or just stay put? But after a couple of years, we felt we weren't supposed to sell our building—and the reality was we didn't have the money to purchase or rent one in the Numbers anyway. Besides, there were no suitable properties available. Our hearts were still burdened for all the displaced people, but what could we do? So we just said, "God's will be done," and left the idea alone.

I'm a person who loves to pray. But one day I had a busy morning, and I really didn't get a chance to spend time with the Lord as I like. So when I made it to the church, instead of going into my office, I snuck into our conference room to pray. Sitting at one of the folding tables in the room, I pulled out my Bible to read a bit and got an idea. I decided to write one Bible verse on the whiteboard in the room and pray through it. I turned the table to face the board and, in big bright orange letters (because that was the only marker in the tray that wasn't dried out), I wrote out Jeremiah 33:3 (NIV): "Call to me and I will answer you and tell you great and unsearchable things you do not know." I prayed that one verse for about an hour. When I finished, I got up out of the chair to go to my office, but I sensed the Spirit of God telling me to sit and be still. So I sat back down and quieted my heart before the Lord. After I sat for about ten minutes in silence, God spoke to my heart: "Watch me do the impossible." I had no idea what the impossible was, but faith and expectation were ignited in my heart. I was so happy, I called my wife on the phone and told her what had happened.

A few weeks went by and nothing out of the ordinary was happening. Then one day I got a call from one of our elders, and he told me, "Pastor, there is a 'for sale' sign on the Walgreens store on 162nd and Glisan." Before I even realized what I was saying, I told him we should buy it! The store sits on one-and-a-half acres of land in the city, and it is centrally located in the Numbers—a prime place for a church. We pulled a quick meeting together with other decision makers in our church and decided to go for it. We found out the building was selling for 1.75 million dollars, which is an unbelievable price for that type of property. In fact, the owners still owed 2.3 million dollars on the property, but they just wanted to unload it. We decide to go for it, but (problem alert!) even though the price was great, we still didn't have the money.

We had our realtor call and set up a time when we could talk with the owners. The property was owned by a business that owned shopping centers throughout the Northwest. We ended up talking with their CFO, their realtor, and their business manager. Their first question was what we planned to do with the property. My response was, "We're going to create a place that will help families and better the community. We're going to open a church." Then he asked how we were going to pay for it: "Do you have cash? Are you preapproved for a loan? Will you raise the money quickly?" I answered all those questions positively in the negative: "No, no, and no!" So he asked again how we would pay for the property. I prayed, "Lord, help us!" Then I got the idea to tell him the story of how we acquired our other property, and I told him I thought we could do it again. He said okay and that they would call us back the next day.

The next day they called us back and said, "This is very untraditional, and usually we don't do this, but you all seem really sincere, so we are going to give you an opportunity to buy the building." Whoever heard of such a thing! But God was in the process of surprising us. We signed the contract and had to come up with the money in forty-five days. Honestly, I figured we could get a loan from our bank. We had been good patrons for over twenty years, but they denied us. We went to several other banks and they denied us too. I guess we were property rich and cash poor. Our time was getting short, and we were on the verge of losing the real money we put down. An international convenience store chain was ready to buy the property (in fact, they made an offer the day after we signed the contract). So we knew they had a well-qualified buyer waiting in the wings in case we couldn't come up with the money!

We were desperate and didn't know what to do. Someone gave the name of a guy who they thought might help. When I called him, he asked me what house I wanted to buy. I told him that we were trying to buy a piece of commercial property, not residential. He told me he couldn't help with that but gave me the number to a bank. Reluctantly, I called, and I got ahold of the person I needed to talk with. I told her about our church and what we were trying to do, and she said, "I don't know how you got our number, but you called the right place." We set a time for her to come out and look at our Williams Street property. When she was leaving, I asked, "Well, what do you think?" Her response floored me. She said, and I quote, "This looks like a God thing to me!" I had never had a banker say that to me.

Once we got down to the details of the loan, we were told that we would have to raise four hundred thousand dollars for the loan to work, and we only had about a couple of months to do it. Our congregation had never raised that type of money in two months, especially in the summer. But by God's grace, it all came in—every penny. We even had a church in our city out of the blue give us a fifty-thousand-dollar check. Everything looked great, and the building in the Numbers was going to be ours for the glory of Jesus Christ. But then we hit a snag—a big snag!

The day we were supposed to close, the bank called and said they couldn't do the loan unless we had a person in our church with a million dollars in property that could be put up as collateral. The problem was due to one of our parking lot leases. They would not give the bank first position, and the bank was not willing to take the risk of being in second place. Well, we didn't have anyone in our congregation who fit that bill. I told her that was the case, and she said, "Okay, I'll call you back."

I had a funeral to perform that day, but ten minutes before it started, she called back. She told us that her boss said that if we could come up with one hundred thousand dollars, they could go forward with the loan. One of our team members had been listening in on the conversation, and both of us fell on the floor and cried out to God. Where could we get that kind of money in four hours? While I was on the floor, the Lord reminded me of a conversation I had with a man while we were trying to raise the initial monies. He had said to me, "I can't help you now. Only ask me if you really, really need something." So, I called him and said, "We really, really need something! We need a hundred thousand dollars in less than four hours." He said he would talk with his wife. In minutes he called back and said, "You got the hundred thousand." I was relieved until after the funeral. As soon as I was finished, I received another call from the bank saying to remember to bring a twenty-thousand-dollar check for closing. But we were broke—we did not have the money. Our elders were at the funeral, so when they found out what was going on, we had a quick meeting to figure out what we could do. But we came up with no solution. We went into the meeting with no clue as to what to do, and we left the meeting even more clueless.

Circumstance would have it that my dad was at the funeral that day and was feeling sick, so he went into my office and lay on the couch—something he never did, nor has he done since. He saw me pacing back and forth, so he told me to come over for a moment because somebody wanted to talk to me on the phone. I told him I couldn't talk right now. Then he pulled the pop's move on me, saying, "Boy, come get this phone." So I went and took the call. The gentleman on the phone said, "What's going on and what do you need?" I told him we needed twenty thousand dollars in less than an hour. He too said, "Let me talk to my wife." By the time he called back, I was at the title company without the money. But then I received a text from our administrator saying the money was there. And so we bought the building to start a church in the Numbers.

The surprise didn't stop there. When we met with the city to tell them our plans for the church, they helped us tremendously. This is unheard of! They told us that once the plans were finished, they would sign off on them in two weeks—and they did just that. Even the contractor for the remodel wanted to help the church, so he donated his services.

Jeremiah 33:3 (NIV) says, "Call to me and I will answer you and tell you great and unsearchable things you do not know." And the Lord spoke to my heart, saying, "Watch me do the impossible." And we watched him do just that! But this isn't only about property.

On the property we purchased, there was a shrine with candles, flowers, little stuffed animals, and so forth. We didn't know what it was, and we didn't want to be insensitive and move it right away. When we started the demo on the building, a White guy in his mid-forties started coming around asking how he could help. We let him help, and when the remodel was finished, he told us his story. The shrine on the property was in remembrance of his son, who was shot and killed on the property in that very place. From that spot, the young man called his father and spoke his last words as he entered into eternity. During one of our first services in the new facility, the father accepted Christ. He was so happy that God had sent something good—a church—to the awful place where his son was murdered.

See, God didn't surprise us just so we could get money and acquire a building. He surprised us because he loves people and he will do anything to reach them. God's surprise enabled us to have a church in two locations. We retained our campus in the moved neighborhood, which is now worth thirty times what we originally paid for it. And we now have another church located in the area where the majority of our displaced neighbors have relocated. We could have never imagined that God would work in such an incredible way to empower us to serve both our current and our moved neighborhood.

Though this story might make it seem like this process was a piece of cake, that was not the case. We tried to buy and lease buildings in that area for several years only to be let down every time. On one occasion we had thought we landed a deal to buy a complex that would have worked great for our church. We figured we would just sell our current campus and move everything to where the people who once lived in our neighborhood are now. The deal was going great, and we were starting to get excited about the new ministry possibilities. We were moving forward until the agent abruptly performed a disappearing act. He stopped communicating with us—no phone calls, texts, or emails. It was the craziest thing, and it didn't make any sense. After weeks of trying without success to reach him, we stopped trying. We discovered months later the reason he ditched us was that he leased the property to his cousin. All that time and effort we had put into making that deal work, only to get sucker-punched in the gut by nepotism. What a discouraging rollercoaster ride!

During this time we spent many days scratching our heads and wondering where God was in all of this. We were confused. We thought that since this promising deal fell through, and we couldn't find a place to lease, maybe God didn't want us to serve in the area where the people had moved. Maybe we were supposed to focus only on our gentrified neighborhood. We had no answers and we had to wait, which is a trial in and of itself, for God to bring us his surprise. So, the picture of our surprise story is not without its smears and marks.

Yes, there is a lot your church has to work through in a moved neighborhood. And yes, you will have to go through a process and experience some dark days. But never forget who is on the throne. There may be some rough sailing, but God may have a few navigational surprises in store for you. Then all you will have to do is watch him do the impossible. Amen!

CONCLUSION

As I said in the beginning, this book is not written by a pro but by a fellow sojourner who is in the process of figuring out how to navigate a church in a moved neighborhood in a way that is faithful and honoring to Jesus Christ. My prayer is that you understand that you are not alone in this situation but know there are others who are facing and working through the same struggles you are. I pray that a ray of hope has entered your heart so that you understand you have options and a moved neighborhood does not mean the demise of your church. It may be hard, but that difficulty does not mean the end. I pray your church will take the time to heal and work its way through the process. Know that while you are going through your process, Jesus is with you every step of the way. I pray that your vision of God grows brighter, bigger, and bolder, and that your identity as a church is fortified and unshaken while your mission burns like a fire in your heart. I pray that you will know exactly what ministry steps your church should take to engage the community and that God will surprise you in ways that will bless the socks off your church and neighborhood.

NAVIGATING THE MOVE

If you have an inkling that change is needed in your church, here are a few final navigation tips for your journey. Here I'll share with you the process that the Spirit of God walked our church through to help make us pliable enough to change.

Clarify. The first thing we had to do was *clarify* what needed to be changed. So we identified three areas. The first was our church's mindset. Our congregation had a bit of the "Hatfields and McCoys" mentality. It was us against the new neighbors. We had to address that mindset and change it. Second, our culture needed to change. Blackness is the taproot of our church, but our neighborhood is now predominately White. So, we had to change some of the big furniture pieces in the church—our music, dress, communication style, and length of service. We incorporated non-gospel-sounding songs in the worship mix, and we stopped using most of the church lingo that only we knew. Third, we changed the assimilation process in our church. We used to have a linear process for integrating people into the church, but now we have developed a process that allows people to immerse themselves in the life of the church at multiple points and places. This process is way more in sync with the ethos of the neighborhood.

So, determine what areas the Spirit of God wants you to change. Identify the changes and clarify them so everyone knows what you are working on.

Convene. Change requires a plan. Trying to change without a plan creates mayhem. Take it from a pro—I know. I've already created enough mayhem for all of us. Planning can be time-consuming and tedious, but taking the time to plan is a great investment in the future of your church. You know your church—its temperament, fears and strengths. Keep these in mind as you craft your plan. Pull together your leadership team or progressive stakeholders in the church to help with this process. Keep it simple, doable, and to the point. Conceptualize in a way that the congregation can understand and call the play. Lay out what you are working to change and clearly identify your plan of action for making those identified changes.

Don't be afraid to try out-of-the-box ideas. One thing we explored was leasing our Williams Street campus to a developer to build affordable housing. Since housing is so expensive in Portland, and a shortage exists, we thought about how our resources could be best used to serve the community and further the mission of the church. The plan was to develop two hundred apartment units for low-income families and also create a space where we could keep a presence in the neighborhood and do church. This would have benefited the church too by giving it a long-term income stream and a long-term presence in the gentrified neighborhood by maintaining ownership of the land. We spent a considerable amount of time trying to figure this out, but due to the Covid-19 pandemic and the present market conditions, we decided not to go that route. My point is, when you plan, be creative, and if something doesn't work, try something else.

Communicate. Make sure the congregation knows what is going on. Have conversations and listen to their feedback. Preach about it and put out publications, both physical and electronic. Develop talking points so the message is clear to everyone. Your goal should be to not leave anyone behind. Communication is key, and if for some reason someone doesn't want to follow, at least it won't be because they were unaware or failed to understand what was going on. You clearly told them.

Conflict. Expect conflict to happen, so thicken your skin and prepare for it. When we began to make some of the changes in our church, we might as well have played the song, "Who Let the Dogs Out?" You would have thought I was asking people to donate both their kidneys! Some members were saying, "Why do we need to change? I'm tired of changing for everybody. Let them change for us!" Some people just withdrew emotionally, and I knew I was on their hit list. We even had people leave the church because they didn't like the music, and they protested the more timely service. They said we were grieving the Holy Spirit and stopping him from working in the church.

My point is, expect conflict. If you have none, praise Jesus! But if you do, stay in a spirit of love and gently try to bring people along through the process. However, do not—I repeat, do not—allow guilt or condemnation to weigh you down. You need your strength to create change, not to carry the guilt put on you by disgruntled people.

Celebrate. Celebrate your victories along the way. One thing we did when we changed our assimilation process was throw a big spaghetti feed. That morning we put tables in the sanctuary, the foyer, and our fellowship area. We had cool centerpieces on the tables, and we had festive balloons and colored lights shining throughout the building. That morning we had a short service, and we all ate and celebrated our new Immersion Life Strategy with one another, and it was a blast. When you celebrate, it doesn't have to be a big affair. It can be as simple as patting someone on the back and letting them know you appreciate all they're doing to help go where God is leading. Cups of coffee, cards, hugs—all work well to celebrate the difficult work of change. Like Mary Poppins sang, "A spoonful of sugar helps the medicine go down." Celebration is that medicine!

Commit. Lastly, stay committed to the process of change. Stick it out to the end. Don't quit or stop too soon. The dividends your church will reap will far outweigh the sweat and tears you've poured into the process. Also, stay committed in the sense that you establish a culture of healthy change in your church. Change is not a one-and-done activity. To stay in sync with God, change will be the norm. So make the commitment for the long haul because change will forever be with you—ugh!

Despite the work navigating your church will require of you, take heart, my fellow sojourner. You will get up off the mat, rise to your feet, and recapture your identity and mission. You will develop a clear vision of the awesomeness of God and fulfill your destiny as the church of Jesus Christ. You are here, your church is here, for such a time as this. God will help you every step of the journey. And not only will he help you—he will surprise you too. Blessings!

RELATIONAL JUMP STARTERS

A t the age of twelve I was fascinated with motor stuff—mini-bikes, motorcycles, go carts, you name it. One dream that I had was to make my own motor go-cart and whiz around the neighborhood on it. On one occasion, while I was visiting my grandpa, I noticed he had an old lawnmower in the garage that he was no longer using. My mind started working, and I thought if I could get that engine, I would be one step closer to building my ride. "Gramps," I said, "can I have the engine on that lawnmower?"

"Son," he said, "the engine is broke. You don't want that." But I persuaded him otherwise, and he gave it to me. When I got home, I took the engine over to my buddy Norman's house. He had more tools than I did. We changed the oil, put new gas in the tank, and pulled the starter cord—and nothing happened. For two more days we were unsuccessful until one of us got the bright idea to put a new sparkplug in the engine. Once the sparkplug was replaced, we pulled the cord, and the engine sputtered. We pulled it again, and it sputtered a bit more. We were getting very hopeful by now. The third time was the charm: we pulled the cord, and *vroom!* We shouted and jumped all over Norman's garage. We were overjoyed to hear the engine roaring like a lion.

Throughout the country, a number of churches have had in-novative ideas to minister to their changed neighborhoods. These ideas may serve as a sparkplug for your church to help get its engine roaring down the streets of the neighborhood. Here's a brief description of a few churches and some of the practical ways they are reaching into their communities.

JOHN WESLEY FREE METHODIST CHURCH (INDIANAPOLIS, INDIANA)

John Wesley Free Methodist Church, a fifty-five-year-old church located in Indianapolis, Indiana, was for years a predominately Anglo suburban church. Throughout the years the core members of the church had aged, and the neighborhood around the church had grown to be more diverse. The new population was composed mostly of Hispanics, African Americans, and Africans. Pastor Kenny Martin said he realized the church was dying because the aging congregation was at a loss as to how to adapt to the changing community. So Pastor Martin led the church through a process of change, and it is now a melting pot of multiple generations and different ethnic groups. Here are some ideas from their experience.

Observation trips. Pastor Martin understood that the church could never see what it should look like now by staring at the inside walls of John Wesley Church. Pastor Martin told me of a time when he went to Walmart and just watched and listened. He saw people of all shades and colors, and he heard multiple languages being spoken. He said in his heart, "Lord, that is what JWFC should look like."

Relationships with people in the community. Pastor Martin says building relationships with people in the community is not a matter of "cold calling." He discovered there were people within the congregation who had good relationships with individuals and groups in the new neighborhood. So they identified those relationships and sought ways to serve those people.

Special Sunday school for those who spoke other languages. They focused on those who spoke Spanish and Swahili.

Youth pastor from Kenya. They hired a young man from Kenya already popular in the community to attract families.

African and Hispanic services. One of the members of John Wesley Church had a good relationship with a few people of the African community surrounding the church. As the church nurtured a relationship with individuals who the existing parishioner knew, they ended up starting a service to reach the African community. The result was that a number of people in the African community started coming to the church. In addition, they started a Spanish-speaking service as well.

Food pantry. The economic challenges the neighborhood now faces make it hard for people to maintain the necessities of life. To help with this, JWFC opened a pantry to help people meet their basic food needs. They also provided clothes and toys for kids.

Mentoring. The mentors work with individuals in the neighborhood who need to do community service. This forged relationships with the person and with their family.

English as a second language classes. The church holds classes to help immigrants in their neighborhood learn English. They also tutor elementary students.

CITY GATE INTERNATIONAL CHURCH (HARLEM, NEW YORK)

City Gate is a multicultural church that has been located in Harlem for over forty years. Pastor Alvin Torres has been a part of the church for sixteen years and the senior pastor since 2004. Currently, the church is composed primarily of Latinos, African Americans, and Puerto Ricans. In 2010, a housing crisis intensified as gentrification pushed Hispanics and African Americans out due to sharp increases in brownstones and even housing projects for those with moderate incomes. In the church, the cultural changes, economic tensions, and gang war crises produced an instability as members had to move out of the area or in with other family members. The instability of housing scattered the congregation, which now travels distances from New Jersey, the Bronx, and Westchester County. Many of the tools Pastor Torres uses today he learned as an elder of this same church when New York faced the intense, back-to-back crises of 9/11 and Hurricane Sandy.

Bivocational opportunities. Pastor Torres is a bivocational pastor. His other job is teaching elementary children in the community, and he emphasizes the power that comes from a face-to-face connection in the neighborhood.

Block festivals. The church holds block festivals, which are popular in Harlem, where streets are closed down and cultural music, dance, and food are presented. These are a favorite in the community. Greeters greet participants in their own language. Toward the end of the event, multicultural worship brings everyone to a unified focus.

Street prayer. The church has teams trained to go out on the streets to pray for people who want or need prayer. The team is multicultural and multilingual so they can pray and partner with those of the same culture.

Food outreach. This service is provided on heavily populated city street corners where substance abuse is rampant. A team of twelve to fifteen people prepares the food and sets up the tables and prayer booths. Often, trained intercessors move more freely among those who are not able to navigate to tables and prayer booths.

Good Friday service. This is their signature service of unity featuring the seven stations of the cross—each in a different language—which ends in a unified worship service in which they sing songs in different languages.

Multilingual greetings. In each church service, Pastor Torres greets people in their own language. He has worked on his own language skills to do so.

Street concerts and prayer circles. When street violence was increasing, they put on "Young People's Concerts" on the neighborhood streets.

On a post-Covid note: Pastor Torres has recently been asked to be a part of a group of pastors that meets with the New York police force in order to talk about creative ideas. Pastor Torres says, "We are still working on them to pray!"

FREEDOM FOURSQUARE CHURCH (GRESHAM, OREGON)

Freedom Foursquare was a new church plant in the Rockwood area of Gresham, Oregon, in 2002. It was planted by a team from East Hill Church, pastored by Dave and Kelly Pauli.

The church had to change locations in March 2005. Though the location was only a few miles from the original one and still in the Rockwood area, the change proved to be a major one. The first immediate difference was the change from a relatively stable neighborhood to a very unstable one. Within the first eight weeks, seven cars were stolen or broken into during the church services. Members, who were used to a more traditional (and secure) service, began to drift away. Pastor Pauli and his wife accepted that, though they were in the same area, the neighborhood was radically different than their original one. Pastor Pauli says, "It wasn't so much that the neighborhood around our church changed as it was that we, the church, moved into a new neighborhood. We quickly realized that a traditional church service would not cut it." The culture surrounding the church was multicultural, homeless, addicted, and primarily low-income, single parents. Pastor Pauli realized that most of the people in the church's neighborhood had no church background and would not know how to "do church." Initially as the church gained some footing in the community, they went through a "long period of throwing events." Here are some of their navigational strategies.

Block parties. Refreshments were served and prayers were offered at prayer booths.

Festivals. These were thrown in the church's big parking lot where music, prayer, food, and clothing were provided.

Attracting like-minded people. The events not only alerted neighborhood people to the fact that a church that provided for basic needs was available, but it also did something the Paulis didn't expect. It attracted those who wanted to serve the disenfranchised. People who wanted to minister began attending the church, and ministry teams began to take shape.

Serving other organizations. When a family shelter was built down the street from the church, food and clothing were taken to the families there. This is when Pastor Pauli's "event mindset" changed to a "church lifestyle" strategy: "The shelter housed these families from 7 p.m. to 7 a.m. These families had nowhere to go during the day, nowhere to shop for food, so we had to build new strategies, but in doing so, we as a church began developing a lifestyle mindset." That was eight years ago, and it is still present today.

Sunday breakfasts. Every Sunday breakfast is served before the sermon. And, if anyone needs clothing, the church has a clothes closet.

Food pantry. They built a food pantry that is open at regular hours so people can come and shop. They reach out to the low-income apartments surrounding the church as well as the homeless to let them know that this is available to them.

Celebrate recovery. They began a program for the addicted so sobriety can be attained.

Christmas parties. They throw Christmas parties for families, kids who don't have families, and adults who have nowhere to go. They also put on plays, so if people want to join in that way, they can do something fun.

Prayer groups. This ministry requires committed workers and prayer warriors. Prayer teams who pray before, during, and after the service are trained.

City prayer groups. During the height of the gang wars eight years ago, a dead body lay across the steps leading into the entrance of the church. Pastor Pauli called pastors in the area together weekly to pray. This group still meets regularly.

Need awareness. As mental illness and homelessness continue to increase in the area, the church added a short service that includes breakfast. Though this a simple gesture in the face of a massive need, this allows the congregation to build relationships with the less transient attendees and creates a bridge of trust to offer more help.

CROSSOVER CHURCH (CHESTERFIELD, VIRGINIA)

Crossover is a twenty-one-year-old church located in rural Virginia. The church is a mixed congregation of Whites and Blacks. Pastor Kevin Meade said over the last three years new housing developments for middle-class and upper-middle-class families have been built around the church. Though the developments have not affected the racial composition of the church or their neighborhood, the economic status of the residents has changed. This has forced the church to rethink its outreach strategies and work hard to find the underserved within their community. These are some of the things Crossover Church does to reach their changed neighborhood.

Children's church. With all the families moving into the new developments, having something great for the kids is important. So they have worked hard to make their church kid friendly.

Serve day. On the fifth Sunday of the month, they have just a short worship service and then serve lunch to first responders in the community and get to know them.

Feeding the homeless teens. Even though the affluence is present, so are homeless teens. The church finds the homeless teenagers in their area to make sure they have something to eat.

Care packages. They provide care packages for individuals in their community who are transitioning out of correctional facilities.

School partnership. The church partners with one of the local schools to make sure the teachers and students never run out of supplies. Also, they give backpacks to the school so the less fortunate students in the schools can carry food home to their families in an inconspicuous manner.

SHILOH CHURCH (OAKLAND, CALIFORNIA)

Shiloh Church is a fifty-five-year-old multigenerational congregation with people from zero to 104 years of age. The church's ethnic composition is made up of over forty different nations. Pastor Javier Ramos says that the neighborhood, which was once the "hood," has undergone major changes. Houses that once sold for one hundred thousand dollars are now selling for nine hundred thousand dollars. Two-bedroom apartments that once went for one thousand dollars a month are now renting for three thousand dollars and above. For years the ministry of Shiloh was deeply woven into the neighborhood and the community, and it still is. But now they are facing the challenge of how to connect with their new neighbors. Pastor Ramos is upbeat about the challenges the church is facing and says these are some of the ways the church is reaching out to the community.

Connecting to people where they are. For years the church has had an incredible college called Shiloh Bible College, but they changed the name to Shiloh Pathways. Due to the name change alone, they had more people from the church and the city sign up for classes. It removed a barrier that kept people from participating.

Feeding the community. They have the second or third largest food pantry in the city. During the Covid-19 pandemic, they have given away five hundred thousand pounds of food. They also partner with restaurants to provide cooked meals to people.

Back to school help. They provide backpacks filled with school supplies. This year they gave away fifteen hundred packs to children in the city.

Night of healing. On the first Sunday night of the month, the church goes to city hall and prays for the city. Since they have begun this outreach, over twenty churches have joined them, and other are constantly coming aboard.

Encouraging connection with neighbors. One of the questions Pastor Ramos repeatedly asks the church is, "Who are you having dinner with?" By encouraging the congregation in this way, organic connections are forming and opportunities to share Jesus are happening.

Creative youth ministry. Shiloh created a number of online activities to engage youth in the community. They even rented a drive-in theater and showed a movie for the teens in the neighborhood.

MT. VERNON BAPTIST (DURHAM, NORTH CAROLINA)

Mt. Vernon Baptist is a historic African American Church. The church was founded in 1886 on land bought for three hundred dollars from W. T. Blackwell, the tobacco industrialist. The church for decades has been a centerpiece in the African American community. One person has been a member for ninety-five years—her parents are the ones who founded the church.

In Durham, gentrification has decimated the African American community and has displaced the majority of Mt. Vernon's members. Reverend Jerome Washington says that since gentrification has taken place, very few members live in the community. The majority have to drive in to attend church. Reverend Washington said, "This is the first time not one child from C. C. Spaulding (the neighborhood grade school, named after a Durham's influential African American forefather) is at this church. . . . The neighborhood has shifted and changed so much, there's no child from the school a half-mile away."[1] Mt. Vernon Church is committed to staying in their location and not moving. Here are some of their strategies for doing so.

Land banking. The church has purchased all the property surrounding the church so they can have control over what happens.

Nonprofit endeavors. The church has an established a credit union for members and created other nonprofit entities for land development.

Capital improvements. The church is currently raising money through a capital campaign to upgrade the buildings' technology and facade.

Commitment to stay. According to Reverend Washington, "In the African-American church, the church is more than a building. It is a safe place, a sanctuary, a refuge and more. It is not easy for a congregation to leave a building in the African-American Church. It was built often by people who did not own a home, but they own a church. It's more than opening the doors on Sunday. . . . It was the one place you got affirmed, and is still one place we get affirmed more than anywhere else."[2]

CHRISTIAN INTERNATIONAL CHURCH
(LINCOLN PARK, NEW JERSEY)

Christian International is a twenty-nine-year-old church located in the suburbs in a very affluent area. Pastor Eric Butler says that much development is occurring in their area due to money being released from the government for construction. They are building new roads and new condo complexes around their property. Right next to their community is an urban area called Paterson. Here are some of the things they're doing.

Community center. The church is working with strategic partners to build a community center where they teach life skills and build community resilience and cohesiveness. This will also be a place to share the gospel and do ministry training. The center is almost completed.

Ministry to first responders. Each year the church hosts a community breakfast for all branches of first responders and their families. This has enabled the church to develop great relationships with the people who perform these courageous jobs. They give them plaques of appreciation for their service, and someone shares a motivational message to thank them.

Ministry to kids' sports teams. They host a large Christmas program for a Pop Warner football team and their cheerleaders. The age range of the children is from five to sixteen. The program is a huge celebration to bless the kids and honor the coaches. The church's music, drama, and arts departments help make the time extra special.

Prayer times. CIC has conducted prayer times where the congregation simply goes out into the community and prays. They pray for the people and ask God's blessing over the entire community.

Outdoor events. They have hosted gospel events in their parking lot where the community is invited to come out, and they have great music and share the gospel with their neighborhood. One recent event had several hundred people present.

LIFE CHANGE CHURCH (PORTLAND, OREGON)

You are already familiar with our story of neighborhood change, so here are some things we are doing to make inroads into our new neighborhood.

County partnership. We've worked with Multnomah County to help address the health needs of seniors in our church and our community. We have functions where the church is open for seniors in the community to come and learn about healthy eating and living.

Old-school inviting people to church. Occasionally, we have a small team of people walk the streets and give passersby one of our church info cards, and they invite them to church. They meet people and connections are made. Every once in a while, someone comes.

Culturally specific literature. We created a little book called *Friendly Joe's Guide to Kinder Portland*. One of the things we noticed about our new hipster neighborhood was people were not as kind as before. So we developed a little nonreligious book that talked about making the city a kinder place. The book was a smash—the libraries, coffee shops, the neighborhood grocery stores, churches, and people all over distributed them. We even got a spot on the local news to talk about the booklet.

Utilizing our building. Businesses, schools, and organizations need space to meet. So we allow them to use space in our building. When they come, we treat them like royalty, making sure they know they are welcomed. We have developed some good inroads into the community just by using our building as a tool.

Parking lot parties. We've held parties in our parking lot with food, games, and music. People from the neighborhood stroll in and meet the congregants and have a good time. We also do trunk-or-treat parties, and parents and kids who have never been on our premises show up.

Just inviting people to come. One thing the people in our church do is invite people to come to church. Sure, not everybody who comes enjoys the experience or stays. But there are those who come back, and their lives are impacted by Jesus Christ.

Affordable housing advocacy. We have supported community efforts to advocate and create affordable housing for poorer remaining families in the community. And we have spoken up in city agencies about the impact of gentrification on the welfare of the community.

Community symposiums. We have held a few community discussions on gentrification where we bring in developers, city officials, and community leaders to discuss the issues. It provides a great time to foster conversation and understanding.

Hopefully, this list of churches and their activities ignite a spark someplace in your heart. By no means is this a comprehensive list. There are many other ways churches can impact their neighborhoods. Churches can work and fight to change policies that perpetuate gentrification. They can partner with other churches to marshal their strengths to address and meet neighborhood needs. Churches can participate in community organizing and work with other like-minded organizations to work together for the welfare of the city. Churches can even plant or start satellite churches in another area of the city. The sky is the limit, and your creativity can be limitless. Don't put yourself in a box thinking you have to be or do like anyone else. However, if something is resonating with you, go for it! Once your church has figured out what it wants to do, pull the starter cord and get moving. Remember, God still does great things with small beginnings.

God is ultimately leading your church in this neighborhood transition, and you never know what he has up his sleeve for your church and your neighborhood. But I tell you what—it is amazing!

NAVIGATION GUIDE

DISCUSSION QUESTIONS

The purpose of *Who Moved My Neighborhood?* is to help pastors, teachers, leaders, and churches *faithfully* navigate the treacherous terrain of a changing neighborhood—a moved neighborhood. These navigational questions are designed to facilitate group discussion to help fulfill that purpose. They provide a means for your congregation to interact with one another and the material in the book so that through your interactions together, your church can form a map of sorts that will help you effectively navigate your new neighborhood together.

To prepare for each session, each participant should read the required chapters, then reflect and pray over the questions prior to the group gathering. Encourage everyone to participate in the group discussion. You are all on this journey together and everyone's input matters.

Navigation Session 1: Chapters 1–3

1. Has your church's neighborhood moved? How do you know?

2. What demographic shifts are you noticing in your neighborhood?

3. How have the economics (e.g., real estate prices, cost of living) changed in your neighborhood?

4. How do these changes affect God's concern for your church?

5. Do you think a church in a moved or gentrified neighborhood is in need of healing? Is your church in need of healing?

6. Do you think a church heals thorough a process? Why or why not?

7. What are some of your fondest memories of how your neighborhood used to be?

8. Why is it important to remember aspects of your old neighborhood?

9. How does it make you feel when you talk about your old neighborhood?

10. What values are a part of your old "regular"? And what can you do as a church to make sure you never lose them?

Navigation Session 2: Chapters 4–6

1. What once familiar spaces in your community have become unfamiliar?

2. When did you first start to recognize changes taking place in your neighborhood?

3. When these changes were taking a place, were you aware or in a fog?

4. Discuss a few ways the church can become more aware of the movement taking place in its neighborhood.

5. Would you say your church has been hit by the force of a blow caused by gentrification or a moved neighborhood?

6. The exiles in Babylon hung up their harps on the poplar trees and refused to sing. How would you say the blow has affected your church community?

7. What can your church do to overcome the trauma caused by the blow?

8. Why do you think it is a natural response to try to reconstruct what was lost in your neighborhood?

9. What frustrations do you feel when you realize you can never make everything the way it once was?

10. What are a few things you can reconstruct in your moved neighborhood? And what can you do to rebuild them?

Navigation Session 3: Chapters 7–9

1. Be honest. Do you have anger over what has happened in your neighborhood, and have you been able to express it in a healthy way?

2. What is it about the changes that angers you the most?

3. How can you as a church provide a safe environment for your anger to be expressed?

4. Do you feel that having a means and environment to express your anger is necessary? Why or why not?

5. Would you say reconciling with the changes in your neighborhood is an easy or hard task? Why?

6. How does the price Jesus paid to reconcile you to God impact your willingness and need to reconcile your heart with the changes in your neighborhood?

7. What steps will you have to take to experience reconciliation as individuals and as a church?

8. What new and fresh opportunities do you see for your church as you prepare to revamp?

9. How can your church together discern God's will for this next season of ministry?

10. Are there specific things your church can do to make sure you are pliable and not inflexible when it comes to change?

Navigation Session 4: Chapters 10–12

1. Why is it important to have a vision of God in the midst of a moved neighborhood?

2. How does the reality of Jesus sitting on the throne affect your theology of being a changed neighborhood?

3. What role does personal surrender and letting go play in your ability to have a fresh vision of God?

4. Why is knowing your identity important, and why do the forces of hell fight it?

5. Describe how you think your old neighborhood helped shape your church's identity.

6. How does Scripture define the church?

7. How can your church reinforce its biblical identity?

8. Why is understanding your church's mission important?

9. As a church, what are your historical and main missional thrusts?

10. Where is the best location for your church to fulfill its mission—where you are or somewhere else? (Note: This is for discussion purposes, not to vote in order to take action. Allow for various opinions. Take it as a chance to listen and learn.)

Navigation Session 5: Chapters 13–14

1. Who is your neighbor? What type of people have moved into your space?

2. Why is having willingness to know and serve your neighbor important?

3. Name some causes of reluctancy that combat our willingness to know and serve our neighbors.

4. What are some ways your church can serve your neighbors?

5. What does Ephesians tell us about God's ability to work through us?

6. How has God surprised your church in the past?

7. How will God's special grace help your church navigate your new journey?

8. What are the next navigational steps your church needs to take in your journey?

9. How can your church strategically pray for its vision, mission, and future?

10. Discuss how your church can affirm its confidence and trust in God to faithfully guide you through all the navigational twists and turns ahead.

NOTES

FOREWORD

[1]Jane Jacobs, *The Death and Life of Great American Cities*, reissue ed. (New York: Vintage Books, 1992), 293.

[2]Daniel Herriges, "Two Simple Rules for Healthy Neighborhood Change," *Strong Towns*, March 4, 2020, www.strongtowns.org/journal/2020/3/4/two-simple -rules-for-healthy-neighborhood-change.

[3]Daniel Herriges, "Calming the Waters: How to Address Both Gentrification and Concentrated Poverty," *Strong Towns*, February 26, 2018, www.strongtowns .org/journal/2018/2/23/calming-the-waters.

[4]Martin Luther King Jr., "Advice for Living," *Ebony*, September 1958, 68, https:// kinginstitute.stanford.edu/king-papers/documents/advice-living-14.

1. WHO MOVED MY NEIGHBORHOOD?

[1]Nikole Hannah-Jones, "In Portland's Heart, 2010 Census Shows Diversity Dwindling," *OregonLive.com*, May 6, 2011, https://sustainablefreedomlab.org /wp-content/uploads/2015/11/Portlands-dwindling-diversity.pdf.

[2]Holly Meyer, "Houses of Worship Do Some Soul-Searching as Their Neighborhoods Change," Religion News Service (via *USA Today*), July 23, 2017, https:// religionnews.com/2017/07/23/houses-of-worship-do-some-soul-searching -as-their-neighborhoods-change/.

2. DISCOVERING THE HEALING PROCESS

[1]C. S. Lewis, *A Grief Observed* (New York: HarperCollins, 1961), 71. Kindle.

4. RECOGNITION

[1]Seema Agnani, "Anti-Displacement Organizing Should Start Here," *ShelterForce*, December 5, 2019, https://shelterforce.org/2019/12/05/anti-displacement -organizing-should-start-here/.

²Juliana Broad, "Fighting Gentrification and Displacement: Emerging Best Practices," *The Next System Project*, February 19, 2020, https://thenextsystem.org /fighting-gentrification-best-practices.

5. REALIZATION

¹Lance Freeman, *There Goes the 'Hood: Views of Gentrification from the Ground Up* (Philadelphia: Temple University Press, 2006), Kindle locs. 1321-27.

7. RAGE

¹Mike Maciag, "Gentrification in America Report," *Governing*, February 2015, www.governing.com/gov-data/gentrification-in-cities-governing-report.html.
²L. Bates, A. Curry-Stevens, and the Coalition of Communities of Color, *The African-American Community in Multnomah County: An Unsettling Profile* (Portland, OR: Portland State University, 2014).

8. RECONCILIATION

¹Andraé Crouch, "I Don't Know Why," by Andraé Crouch, *Classics, Vol. 1*, CGI Records, 1993.
²Brian Libby, "In Growing Portland, the Strategy Is Density Over Sprawl," *New York Times*, December 8, 2015, www.nytimes.com/2015/12/09/realestate/commercial /in-growing-portland-the-strategy-is-density-over-sprawl.html.
³Portland Housing Bureau, "Displacement in North and Northeast Portland: An Historical Overview," www.portlandoregon.gov/phb/article/655460.

10. THE VISION QUESTION

¹T. P. Pearce, "Sovereignty of God," in *The Holman Illustrated Bible Dictionary*, ed. C. Brand et al. (Nashville: Holman, 2003), 1,523.

11. THE IDENTITY QUESTION

¹C. Stevenson et al., "Neighborhood Identity Helps Residents Cope with Residential Diversification: Contact in Increasingly Mixed Neighborhoods of Northern Ireland," *Political Psychology* 40 (2019): 277-95, doi:10.1111/pops.12510.
²Polly Fong et al., "Neighbourhood Identification Buffers the Effects of (De-) gentrification and Personal Socioeconomic Position on Mental Health," *Health & Place* 57 (2019): 247-56.
³Justin Taylor, "O Love That Will Not Let Me Go," *The Gospel Coalition*, August 4, 2010, www.thegospelcoalition.org/blogs/justin-taylor/o-love-that-will-not -let-me-go/.
⁴George Matheson, "O Love That Wilt Not Let Me Go," 1882.

12. THE PURPOSE QUESTION

[1]Holly Meyer, "Houses of Worship Do Some Soul-Searching as Their Neighborhoods Change," Religion News Service, July 23, 2017, https://religionnews.com/2017/07/23/houses-of-worship-do-some-soul-searching-as-their-neighborhoods-change/, emphasis added.

13. THE RELATIONAL QUESTION

[1]Hamil R. Harris, "As Neighborhoods Change, Churches Emphasize Their Roles in Community," *Washington Post*, March 23, 2012, www.washingtonpost.com/local/as-neighborhoods-change-churches-emphasize-their-roles-in-community/2012/03/15/gIQAxll7VS_story.html.

[2]See Mark E. Strong, *Divine Merger: What Happens When Jesus Collides with Your Community* (Downers Grove, IL: InterVarsity Press, 2016), 100-101.

APPENDIX: RELATIONAL JUMP STARTERS

[1]Dawn Baumgartner Vaughan, "Gentrification in Durham: 'We're Not Going Anywhere,' Says Pastor of Historic Black Church," *The Herald Sun*, December 20, 2019, www.heraldsun.com/news/local/article224513355.html.

[2]Vaughan, "Gentrification in Durham."

SCRIPTURE INDEX

OLD TESTAMENT

Genesis
1–3, 97
17:1, 97

Exodus
3:14, 108

Deuteronomy
32:4, 97

1 Samuel
16:7, 20

2 Chronicles
26:4, 95

Nehemiah
1:1-4, 48, 54
2:11-13, 55
3, 55, 56
4:2, 56

Job
14:7-9, 56
42:2, 97

Psalms
90:4, 97
103:8, 97
135:6, 102
137, 45
137:1, 41
137:1-4, 40
139:1-6, 97
139:7-12, 97

Proverbs
8:22-31, 97

Isaiah
6:1-5, 97
6:1-8, 95
61, 118

Jeremiah
29:7, 40
32:17, 97
33:3, 135, 139

Lamentations
3:22-23, 97

Daniel
4:34-35, 102

Habakkuk
1:2, 97
1:3, 65

Malachi
3:6, 97

NEW TESTAMENT

Matthew
4:1, 104
4:1-7, 105
6:33, 97
10:37, 131
11:28-30, 103
16:17-18, 108
19:26, 97
22:39, 127
23:37, 17

Luke
4:18-19, 118
5:36-39, 91
9:54, 74
10:29-37, 128
10:34-35, 130

John
4, 17
10:17-18, 78

Acts
10, 132
10:19-20, 132
10:19-26, 132
10:27-33, 133
10:34-43, 133

Romans
8:5-6, 90
8:26-27, 101
8:35-39, 114
12:2, 86

1 Corinthians
15:14, 78

2 Corinthians
5:14-15, 78

Ephesians
2:8-10, 111
2:11-18, 67
4:11-13, 86
4:26, 64

Philippians
4:5-8, 89

Colossians
3:15-17, 88

Hebrews
4:16, 65
11:21, 94
12:2, 94
13:8, 97

James
1:17, 97

1 Peter
1:15-16, 97
2:9-10, 112
5:11, 97

1 John
4:8, 98
4:16, 98

Revelation
4:1-3, 98
4:8, 97